M000215861

Let everybody praise the LORD!

an exposition of Psalm 107

Let everybody praise the LORD!

an exposition of Psalm 107

D. Martyn Lloyd-Jones

BRYNTIRION PRESS

Unless otherwise stated all Scripure quotations are from
the Authorised (King James) Version.

Cover photograph: Daniel K. Tennant
Cover design: Phil Boorman @ burgum boorman ltd

Published by Bryntirion Press
Bryntirion, Bridgend CF31 4DX, Wales, UK
Printed by WBC Book Manufacturers, Bridgend

Contents

1
Let everybody
praise the LORD

'O give thanks unto the LORD, for he is good: for his mercy endureth for ever. Let the redeemed of the LORD say so, whom he hath redeemed from the hand of the enemy; and gathered them out of the lands, from the east, and from the west, from the north, and from the south.'
(Psalm 107:1-3)

Psalm 107 is obviously a hymn of praise, a song of thanksgiving, of worship and of adoration, and as we look in detail at these first three verses, we must also, at the same time, call attention to the entire psalm and to its message as a whole.

Structure

The structure of this psalm is quite clear; it divides itself up naturally. But here, in these first three verses, we have a kind of introduction. The Psalmist is, as it were, gathering together a great choir which he is going to conduct as they sing this anthem of praise unto God, so he assembles together the various members of his choir who are singing the different parts. He sends out a great invitation; he calls them to come together 'from the east, and from the west, from the north, and from the south'; and he is asking them all to join together in giving thanks unto the Lord. He says, 'Let the redeemed of the LORD say so'. And at once he provides us with the reasons why all these different people coming from different places should come together in this one great anthem.

But then, having done that, he goes on to details. He is not content with merely making a general statement; he wants now to prove that statement. He says that all the redeemed of the Lord will join together in this, even though their experiences, in certain senses, have been different; so he proceeds to give us four samples or illustrations of four different types of experience.

The first group are people who are to be seen wandering in a wilderness seeking 'a city of habitation'. The second group are those who are 'bound in affliction and iron'. The third are those who seem to be pining away in ill-health and on the point of starvation, and the fourth is a picture of those who are on the sea in great waters and in a terrible storm. He gives us detailed descriptions of these four types and of their varying experiences, but in each case, you notice, he uses the same language. He has something to say about every one of the groups, and he says the same thing each time: 'Then they cried unto the LORD in their trouble'; and each time he is able to say, 'and he delivered them out of their distresses' (v.6). So he invites each group by saying, 'Oh that men would praise the Lord for his goodness, and for his wonderful works to the children of men!' (v.8).

Then, having dealt with his four types, his four illustrations, he goes on to show us God's dealings with these people in general. And he concludes with a final word of challenge and of exhortation: 'Whoso is wise, and will observe these things, even they shall understand the lovingkindness of the LORD' (v.43).

Now that is a general analysis of this great and most notable psalm. It is a typical example of Old Testament praise. It is, in a sense, a very characteristic psalm, and I am calling your attention to it because it does, at the same time, present us with a picture of what may be described as true religion. Not every religion is true. There is such a thing as false religion; and nothing is more important for us than that we should be able to differentiate between the two.

So as we study this psalm together, we shall, incidentally, be enabled to do that. Here the blessings that come upon those who are truly related to God are presented to us in this dramatic and pictorial manner. The whole theme is that we should come to know and understand the loving kindness of the Lord; and the man wrote his psalm in order that everybody might come to understand that. He invites all these people to sing this anthem of praise to God in order that those who are not praising God may be arrested and may ask the questions, 'Why are these people praising God? What reason have they for doing this? What is it about them that makes them do so?' They do not do it merely for their own enjoyment; they do it also in order that they may be the means of bringing others into a like knowledge of the loving kindness of the Lord.

So here is a typical statement of the praise of godly people under the Old Testament dispensation. But, of course, it is not only that. It is also a picture of the same praise that goes up out of the minds and the hearts and the souls of the New Testament people. It is the same God in the Old Testament and in the New. The Old Testament saints are members of the same kingdom of God as the saints in the New. Our Lord himself said that those who enter the kingdom in the new dispensation go into the same kingdom as Abraham and Isaac and Jacob (Matthew 8:11). The fathers, he says, belong to the same kingdom. We come into the kingdom under a new dispensation, but we come into the same kingdom. The blessings of the Old Testament, in a sense, are the same as the blessings of the New. It is the same covenant of grace; it is the same gracious God dealing with us. And that is why Christian people throughout the centuries have found that there is no better way of expressing their worship, and their praise especially, than to turn to the Book of Psalms and to read or to sing a psalm together. It is the same spiritual life given by the same God and leading us into the same eternal and everlasting kingdom.

Now in this particular case there is no doubt that the Psalmist had very clearly in his mind the deliverance of the children of Israel from captivity. The message of the Old Testament can be summarised in this way. God's people are in relationship to God, and as long as they live a life of obedience God will shower his blessings upon them. But he has warned them from the very beginning that if they fail to obey him, if they fail to keep in touch with him, he will turn his back upon them for the time being. They will be conquered by enemies; they will be carried away into captivity; they will be scattered out of their land, out of their home which he has given them; and they will be fugitives and wanderers; they will be strangers in a strange land.

He told them that at the beginning, and because, in their folly, they forgot him and disobeyed him and turned their backs upon him, that very thing happened to them. They knew what it was to be strangers in captivity. But there they cried out unto the Lord and he heard them and he brought them back. They were taken captive, some of them by the Assyrians, others by the Chaldeans, and carried far away from Jerusalem into Assyria and into Babylon. But those who cried out were brought back, a remnant returned; and the Psalmist is undoubtedly thinking of this. 'Let the redeemed of the LORD say so', he says, 'whom he hath redeemed from the hand of the enemy; and hath gathered them out of the lands, from the east, and from the west, from the north, and from the south.'

Again, there is no question at all but that that Old Testament history is a perfect portrayal of the New Testament salvation and of that which happens to the Christian in the New Testament. The children of Israel have been brought into being by God, and he has used them as an illustration and an example to the whole world of his way of dealing with mankind. So it is in that way that I want to use this psalm now.

It is good for us to think of these things sometimes in the form of pictures. The doctrine is there very simply and plainly in many places in the New Testament, but let us take this picture. Let us have a look at the gospel in the Old Testament, for it is there everywhere if you have eyes to see it, and you can see it in this delightful pictorial manner that impresses it upon the mind and enables us to remember it.

Praise—the primary note

Now there are, it seems to me, certain great principles taught here. The first is this: the primary and the fundamental note of Christianity, and, therefore, the chief characteristic of the Christian, is the giving of thanks unto God: 'O give thanks unto the LORD, for he is good: for his mercy endureth for ever. Let the redeemed of the LORD say so . . .' Let them say so, says the Psalmist, and he exhorts them and urges them to do this because they have reasons for saying so, as I shall show you.

But first of all we must grasp clearly the primacy for the Christian of this sense of gratitude and of praise to God. This is obviously a very important statement. It is certainly one of the best and the briefest ways in which we can test ourselves in order that we may discover where we are.

Relationship

So let us do that! Are we conscious of that thanksgiving? What is a Christian? Well, obviously, a Christian must be a person who is conscious of a *relationship to God*. You cannot read the New Testament without at once coming to that conclusion. Indeed, as I have already pointed out, this stands out plainly and clearly in the Old Testament also. According to the Bible, there are only two divisions of men and women: we are all of us either godly or ungodly. It is either true of us at this moment that the biggest thing in our lives is our relationship to God, or else it is not.

If you go through the Bible you will find that this is always the way. What is the difference between Cain and Abel? What is the

11

difference between Noah and his family and all the rest of the world? What is it that marks out Abraham? What is the thing that picked him out in that pagan atmosphere in which he was brought up? It was this relationship to God. He was a God-centred man, a man who relied upon God and depended upon him and who had a sense of dependence on and of gratitude to God. And I could take you in the same way right through those Old Testament patriarchs and saints and prophets and all the others. That is always the thing that differentiates them. They have this sense of God; it is what marks them out.

Now if that is true even of the Old Testament, how much more is it true of the New Testament! Christian men and women, by def-inition, are people who believe that they are in this relationship to God in a certain way and for a certain reason. It is not that they live a certain type of life and that they do not do certain things; the first thing about them is that they are concerned about God. And there-fore the thing that is so obvious about all who are not Christian is that ultimately there is no thought of God in their minds, nor in their hearts, nor in their lives.

Gratitude

'O give thanks unto the LORD, for he is good: for his mercy endureth for ever.' Furthermore, Christians are not only concerned about this relationship to God; in their hearts there is a *sense of gratitude*, of thanksgiving, to God. They are anxious to praise him. God is to them the Lord of their lives, and they are conscious of this sense of dependence upon him; they have a sense of the goodness of God. Listen to other psalmists saying, 'Surely goodness and mercy shall follow me all the days of my life' (Psalm 23:6); 'Bless the LORD, O my soul: and all that is within me, bless his holy name' (Psalm 103:1). That is Old Testament.

Now, if that is Old Testament, how much more is this true of the New Testament! And as you turn to it you find that that is its great characteristic. It has often been said, and said truly, that the book of the Acts of the Apostles is the most lyrical book in the world. The thing that characterised the first Christians was that joy which was quite irrepressible. It did not matter what you did with them; you could throw people like Paul and Silas into prison and put their feet fast in the stocks, but you will find that at midnight they 'prayed, and sang praises unto God' (Acts 16:25). It did not matter, I say, what happened to them, there was this joy within them. Their hearts were singing; they were praising God.

And as you read the Epistles you will find exactly the same note. The Epistles were all written, in a sense, just to tell God's people that, whatever may be taking place, they must still go on praising God. They must realise that they are to look upon these adverse conditions in the light of their new relationship to him. So the apostle Paul, in writing to the Philippians, constantly repeats the same thing. He says, 'Finally, my brethren, rejoice in the Lord' (Philippians 3:1). And then he says it again, 'Rejoice in the Lord alway: and again I say, Rejoice' (Philippians 4:4).

And why was the book of Revelation ever written? It was not written primarily, let me assure you, in order that people might be able to work out the date of the end of the world! That is a very grievous misunderstanding of that book. The book of Revelation was written in order that God's people who were passing through terrible persecutions and terrible adversity might still be able to go on rejoicing. It is a book that showed them the ultimate victory of the Lord over Satan and all the other forces. They were to rejoice. It was written for men and women who had been in trouble, and it was meant to help *them*, not some people who were to live about two thousand years later. And so it has been a help to Christian people in every age and in every generation, and if your understanding of the book of Revelation does not help you to rejoice, you are misunderstanding it.

So then, that is obviously the first, the chief and the most characteristic note of the Christian. Christian men and women not only know God and believe in him, they want to thank God. They praise him. They are conscious of God's goodness.

A vital test

Now you see at once what a vital and a valuable test this is. Morality, good as it is, never leads to such a result. A moral man is a very good man. He may indeed be a *very* good man, but as long as he has nothing more than morality he will never be a man who praises God. He may be very correct; he will be. He may be most punctilious. You may not be able to point a finger at him. There may not be a single blot on the copybook of his life. But it is a characteristic of the moral man that he never warms your heart, and that is because his own heart is not warmed. There is no thankfulness there, and that is why an acute thinker like Matthew Arnold—who was not a Christian—was at any rate able to say this: he defined religion as 'morality tinged with emotion'. He was absolutely right there, in a sense. He saw, at any rate, the difference between morality and Christianity. Morality is complete, perhaps; it is correct, yes, but it is cold. There is no emotion there. Even the unbeliever Matthew Arnold, as he read his Scriptures and as he read the history of the church and as he knew something about the lives of the saints, could see that, blind as he was. It is impossible to be a Christian without emotion. Now I am not advocating emotionalism; I am the last man in the world to do so. But I would reiterate again that if there is no emotion in your religion it is not Christian. It is morality.

And, in the same way exactly, the giving of thanks, the offering of praise differentiates Christianity from philosophy. There are many philosophic systems, and many of them are very noble and excellent. They have high ideals, wonderful thoughts. Yes, but philosophy remains in the intellect, and for that reason it, likewise, is always cold. Indeed, if a philosopher begins to display any emotion, his fellow philosophers will not be slow to criticise him. They will begin to say that something has gone wrong with him. The whole art of the philosopher is to be detached, to stand apart. He is the analyst; he looks on; he deals with categories, and he works out his concepts. He must never be lost in it; if he does, he ceases to be a good philosopher. It is this cold, scientific, intellectual detachment. That is philosophy.

So it is in that way essentially different from Christianity. The glory about Christianity is that it takes up the whole person. It is not merely the will, as in morality; it is not merely the intellect, as it is in philosophy; and it is not only and merely the emotion, as it is in certain cults and false religions. No, no; it is the whole man or woman.

An essential feature

But, above all, I want to emphasise that this element of praise is the *absolute essential* in Christianity. Christians are men and women who, before everything else, are conscious that they owe everything to the grace of God. The apostle Paul has put it finally for us in these words: 'But by the grace of God I am what I am' (1 Corinthians 15:10). He owes it all to God. And that is why he praises God.

O, let us examine ourselves! This is the one thing in life and in the world that we cannot afford to take for granted. It is possible for you and for me to have a religion in which we feel no sense of gratitude to God. My religion may be something that I, as it were, carry with me in a bag; it may be something which is nothing more than a kind of self-admiration society. I am glad that I do pay my respects to God and I think I am a good man or woman because I do it. I am really worshipping myself for being good, and not worshipping God.

Never let us confuse church membership with true Christianity. You can be a church member without being a Christian, and if your

Christianity is merely a matter of membership of a church, or even your work in the church, if it lacks this sense of gratitude to God, if it is what *you* are doing and what *you* are, rather than your praise to him, then it is not true New Testament Christianity.

You cannot get away from this. Christians realise that they owe everything to the grace of God in our Lord and Saviour Jesus Christ. And, therefore, it is the first, the fundamental test. Is there praise to God in your heart? Do you feel like responding to the invitation and the appeal of this man: 'O give thanks unto the LORD, for he is good: for his mercy endureth for ever. Let the redeemed of the LORD say so.'? Are you ready to say it? Is there any response in you? Do you find yourself regretting that you do not praise him more? Are you sorry about that? Can you say,

> *Lord, it is my chief complaint*
> *That my love is weak and faint;*
> *Yet I love Thee and adore;*
> *O for grace to love Thee more!*
> William Cowper

Can you say even that much? If you cannot say positively that you are praising God, can you say that you want to? Can you say that you bemoan the fact that you are not doing so more? I think that even that brings you in, for that means that you are praising, that you even want to praise. It is the first and chief characteristic of true Christians. It is not a philosophy they have taken up; it is not a morality that they are practising; it is this sense that they owe everything, all, to God.

Praise—true of all Christians

Then the second principle is that this is something that is true of *all* Christians. Now I want to emphasise this. 'Let the redeemed of the LORD say so,' says the Psalmist, 'whom he hath redeemed

16

from the hand of the enemy; and gathered them out of the lands, from the east, and from the west, from the north, and from the south.'

This is a very important point. Here is a man who is inviting people from different portions and parts of the world to come together; and in spite of all their differences, he is calling them to unite their voices in the one theme. Here is an invitation to all and sundry, as it were, to come together to sing this universal anthem.

I put it like that because of the modern idea about Christianity. We are all such great psychologists these days that we think we can explain away Christianity very simply and very easily. 'Ah,' we say, 'of course there are certain people who are religious, who are Christians, and this is because they happen to have been born like that; they are made like that; they are the religious type. Or, if you like, they have the religious complex. There are these different types of temperament: some people are mercurial, others are pragmatic; some are punctilious—perhaps over-punctilious; others are careless and negligent, "come day, go day". Some are interested in music, art, literature, politics, science, and all those various things. So the human race is divided up like this, and amongst them there is this religious type. And the tragedy, of course, of the past was that the Church used to teach that everybody should be religious. They did not realise; they hadn't the knowledge as we now have, which says that it is all right for some but is not meant for all; it is just for certain types of people.' So the argument goes.

A universal invitation
But this man in sending out his invitation gives the lie direct to this modern theory. He invites them 'from the east and from the west, from the north and from the south'. He says that all these divisions and distinctions are completely irrelevant. They make no difference at all. He is calling men and women who come from entirely different backgrounds to join in the same praise. And that is still

the proud claim and boast of the Christian Church, as it has been throughout the centuries. It does not matter what country a man comes from; it does not matter what is the colour of his skin; it does not matter what his heredity is; it does not matter what his cultural background is; it does not matter what he is temperamentally, what is psychologically; it does not matter what century he belongs to; it does not matter to the slightest extent what his actual experience may be. Still the invitation goes out to all to come together and to unite in the same words and in the same anthem of praise. 'Oh that men would praise the LORD for his goodness, and for his wonderful works to the children of men!' (v.8).

Now this is, to me, one of the most important principles we can ever grasp. You notice that I put the emphasis upon the fact that it does not matter at all how different our experiences may be. Still we come to the same position. There is no standard type of conversion. It does not matter at all what a person's life has been. Let me put it like this. I have known what it is to meet people who have really believed that only certain types of people needed to be converted. I remember once preaching an evangelistic sermon like this in a certain very religious town. I was at the time a minister in a mission church, in a dockland area of South Wales, and I was told that the comment that had been made by a minister in the respectable town was this: 'Now that sort of thing is all right, of course, in his own church, but it is not needed here.'

Indeed, I once heard of a lady sitting even in Westminster Chapel who said, 'This man preaches to us as if we were all sinners.' The idea being, you see, that there are certain people who are sinners and, of course, they need to be converted, they need to be regenerated. But not everybody, not all. In other words, people make a great division and distinction according to the type of experience we have been passing through. Drunkards, of course, need to be converted. Adulterers must be converted. But nice and polite people who have always been brought up in a place of worship, they don't need to be converted! That is the teaching.

A common denominator

But it is not the doctrine of the Bible. The doctrine of the Bible is that whatever your past, whatever your antecedents, whatever your father and mother were, whatever your grandparents were, whatever name you bear, wherever you have been brought up, every man and woman alive needs to be converted, needs to be born again. It is universal: east and west, north and south, all these divisions and distinctions are completely irrelevant. We, all of us, in certain respects, become one when we become Christians.

That is the great contention which is put in this pictorial form as this man assembles his choir. But also, of course, you see it perfectly in the New Testament. Can you imagine twelve men more different than the twelve disciples? Look at the difference between a Peter and a John: John the mystic, the poet, the contemplative; Peter the dare-devil, the activist, the courageous man, the physical man, if you like.

Then look at a man like Paul, who is entirely different from all the others. Look at a man like Nathaniel; look at a man like Andrew. Go through your list. Look at all these men. I say that if you merely apply the canons of psychology, or if you make an analysis of them by your philosophy, you would say that all these men are essentially different. And so they are, and yet they are one in their message, in their praise. They are one in this anthem, in this choir. And it is not only true of them, it is true of the whole subsequent history of the Christian Church.

That is why the reading of biography to me is always such a tonic in this matter. Read the lives of Christian men and women, and you will find that they are people who are by nature entirely different, and yet they all come to the same place. They are all doing the same thing. Of course they are not made like postage stamps, but essentially it is the same experience, it is the same thing to which they testify. They join in the same anthem.

It would be very difficult to imagine two more different people than those two men who were partly contemporaries, Martin Luther and John Calvin. The explosive, volcanic Luther: the careful, precise, logical Calvin. And yet both men joined in doing exactly the same thing. And it is the same with all who stand out in the history of the Church throughout the running centuries.

So let me put my second point again in this way. As the chief characteristic of Christians is that they praise God, so it is the chief characteristic of *all* Christians, of *every* Christian. It does not matter what you are by birth and nature and antecedents. If you come to God in Christ there will be that in you which is in all other Christians. It brings us to a common denominator; it introduces a common factor.

What produces unity?

Let me go on finally to ask this question: What is it that produces this unity? Here is the Psalmist inviting them from north, south, east and west, and he is going to ask them to sing exactly the same thing, the same words. What is it that leads them to do so? What is it that produces this amazing unity? He gives us the answer himself in these first three verses.

The character of God

The first thing is the character of God. 'O give thanks unto the LORD, for he is good: for his mercy endureth for ever.' It is the goodness of God. We do not start with ourselves in Christianity; we always start with God. And it is because people today are so fond of starting with themselves and forgetting God that they lack this unity.

But the Psalmist puts it in the right order. He starts with God, and this is his contention: he says that the moment men and women know God and realise something of who God is and what he is, they will praise him because he is good, because of his character. If you and I are not praising God as we should, there is only one reason for it, and that is that we do not know him. Do you know what is happening in heaven at this very moment? The brightest angelic spirits are there praising God. They are ascribing praise and honour and glory unto the Almighty God. 'Holy, holy, holy, is the LORD of hosts' (Isaiah 6:3). All those angelic choirs are praising God. Why? Well, because he is God. 'The heavens declare the glory of God' (Psalm 19:1). Everything in nature—if we had but eyes to see it—is declaring the glory, the wonder, the greatness of God. And if mankind had not fallen and become subject to sin, everybody would be praising and worshipping God. God made us in order that we might do so, and while man and woman were in the right relationship to God, they did do so.

My dear friend, this is vitally important. Do you know that if you ever find yourself in hell it will be for this reason, that you have not praised God? Now forget all about sin for a moment. Forget all about yourself and your life. Here is the first thing: are you praising God? You were meant to! You were created in order that you might do so. God is to be praised because he is what he is and because he is God, and I know of no more terrible sin than just failure to praise him. And, let me put it bluntly even at the risk of being misunderstood, the reason why the New Testament gives us the impression that the proud Pharisee is the most hopeless person in the universe is just that. The self-righteous, self-satisfied person, according to the Scripture, is an infinitely greater sinner than a drunkard or a prostitute; and for this reason, that there is no atom of praise to God in his life. He is entirely self-satisfied; he spends the whole of his time praising himself.

Look at our Lord's picture of it in the parable of the Pharisee and the publican. Listen to that Pharisee. This is what he says: ' God, I thank thee'—for what? Well, 'that I am not as other men are' (Luke

18:11) 'I am so wonderful!' He does not praise God because God is God. He praises God because he himself is good. He fasts twice in the week; he gives a tenth of his goods to the poor; he is not like this publican, this extortioner; he is a good man. He thanks God for that and, of course, he is not thanking God at all. He is thanking himself. He is telling God about himself. He asks for nothing, he thanks for nothing. The most terrible sin, therefore, is respectability; a reliance upon your religiosity; a reliance upon your morality or upon your right-thinking, or upon anything but the grace of God in Christ.

God is to be praised because he is God, and if men and women are not praising God, that is the essence of sin. They are not ascribing the glory unto God which is due to him because of his majesty, his might, his dominion, his power, his godhead, his eternity. 'O give thanks unto the L<small>ORD</small>, for he is good.' And it is because you and I do not realise this goodness that we fail to thank him: 'for he maketh his sun to rise on the evil and on the good, and sendeth rain on the just and on the unjust' (Matthew 5:45). That is God! The God who sends the seasons one after another and who fructifies the earth; who is blessing men and women in spite of their sin. That is God! And if we knew him we would praise him. He is to be praised because he is good.

The mercy of God
But he gives us another reason for praising him, and that is that 'his mercy endureth for ever', which means that though we have not praised him, and we do not praise him as we ought, he has not finished with us; he has not turned his back upon us; he has looked upon us with mercy and with pity and with compassion.

Look at his mercy with the children of Israel, who turned their backs and went away from him and forgot him and put up other gods and insulted him by worshipping idols. Why did he not blot them out of existence? There is only one answer: 'his mercy endureth for ever'. He bore their evil manners, we are told. But if you would know this mercy of God, look at Christ; look at the babe of Bethlehem; look at the cross. 'God so loved the world that he gave his only begotten Son' (John 3:16). 'His mercy endureth for ever'. Yes! And how does he show this? Well, it is put here for us. We shall deal with it again in detail, God willing, but let me summarise it now as the Psalmist summarises it here in these first three verses. The mercy of God is seen in the fact that he even looks upon us at all. We do not deserve that much. If we had our deserts we would all be blotted out. But God continues to look upon us and upon our world, and then he says, 'Let the redeemed of the LORD say so, whom he hath redeemed from the hand of the enemy; and gathered them out of the lands. . .' What a perfect statement of the gospel!

Redemption
He says that we have been redeemed out of the hand of our enemies. That just means that we have all found ourselves in a condition of distress in this world. We shall see, as we go through this psalm, that it does not matter whether these people are wandering in a wilderness, or sitting helpless in chains in a prison, or dying upon a sick bed, or reeling and staggering like drunken men in the midst of a storm at sea. This is true of all of them: 'They cried unto the LORD in their trouble.' They are in distress; things have gone wrong. They are helpless and hopeless, they cannot do anything; and in their utter helplessness they remember the God they have forgotten and cry out to him for mercy and compassion, and he hearkens unto them and delivers them out of their distresses.

That is common to every Christian, and you cannot be a Christian without knowing that. Christians are men and women who have known themselves in sore distress. They have become desperate about themselves. Do not misunderstand me; if you have not become desperate about yourself, I have no right to tell you that

you are a Christian. Christians are those who have become so desperate about themselves and about their lives that they do not know
what to do. As we are told here, they are at their wits' end; they are
in agony; they do not know where they are. They have been turning over new leaves; they have been making New Year resolutions;
they have been trying to do good; they have been increasing their
subscriptions to good causes. They have been fasting, sweating,
praying, and still they do not know. They are lost.

And in their utter helplessness and hopelessness they have cried
out to the Lord. That is the Christian. Christians are men and
women who have tried everything and exhausted everything and
found them all to fail, and then find the all that they have been
seeking in the Lord Jesus Christ, the Son of God. They have
become desperate and hopeless about themselves, they realise that
they cannot save themselves, and they delight to hear the message
that God has so loved them that he sent his only Son into the world
to rescue them, to die for them, to deliver them, and to reconcile
them to God. 'He delivered them out of their distresses.' He has
redeemed us: 'Let the redeemed of the L<small>ORD</small> say so, whom he hath
redeemed from the hand of the enemy.'

I will describe the enemies later, God willing. But we know
about them, do we not? Lust, passion, jealousy, envy, avarice,
hatred, malice, spite, uncleanness, foulness, perversion. There they
are: the things that get us down and hold us down captive, and we
can never get out of them. The most moral person is perhaps most
tightly in the grip of the enemy. The devil has them most securely
in the fetters of self-righteousness and self-satisfaction. There are
the enemies, and God delivers us out of them.

All Christians have that experience. I do not care what their sin
was; I do not care what form; I do not care what their temperament;
I do not care what their nationality. If they are Christians they have
been desperate, and have found salvation in Jesus Christ alone. So
that all Christians can join in the same anthem, because they are

praising the same God who is good, whose mercy endures for ever, who has redeemed them, yes, and gathered them and brought them to this large and wealthy place in which they have a new nature and a new life and a blessed hope, and the Spirit within them leading them and guiding them; the God who has given them power to overcome sin, has gathered them together and is leading them together in the direction of their everlasting and eternal home.

2
The wilderness

*'They wandered in the wilderness in a solitary way;
they found no city to dwell in. Hungry and thirsty, their
soul fainted in them. Then they cried unto the LORD in their
trouble, and he delivered them out of their distresses. And he led
them forth by the right way, that they might go to a city of
habitation. Oh that men would praise the LORD for his
goodness, and for his wonderful works to the children of
men! For he satisfieth the longing soul, and filleth
the hungry soul with goodness.'*
(Psalm 107:4-9)

As we have indicated, the great theme of this psalm is the praise that is to be offered to God for his goodness. We praise him because he is good and because of the manifestation of his goodness in our salvation. It is praise to God for 'his mercy', which 'endureth for ever'.

In other words, the psalm tells us that salvation comes only from the Lord; so the Psalmist expounds this theme and puts it to us in a number of different ways. It is God alone who is to be praised, because, apart from him, there is no salvation; but in him there is an abundant and a plentiful salvation. And as we were at pains to emphasise, this is for everybody, for all who seek it; for all who become conscious of their need—north and south, east and west, irrespective of temperament, conditions, background, abilities, everything else. It is for all who realise their distress and who are anxious to be delivered out of the hands of the enemy that holds them in such a terrible bondage.

But having laid that down in those first three verses, the Psalmist is not content merely with making a general proposition; he now gives us examples and illustrations. He is like a man who sets down a great thesis and then goes on to prove that thesis, or again (and this is quite a legitimate thing to do with a psalm which is a song), it is like a great symphony. He has his introduction and he tells us what he is going to do. Then he does that in a number of movements, and finally he gathers it all up together at the end. It is indeed, therefore, a most artistic composition and something which calls for our admiration in that sense, in addition to its inherent spiritual truth and value.

So we are now beginning to consider these different cases which the Psalmist puts for our consideration. He has four main examples, and it is generally agreed that these four illustrations are undoubtedly to be used and to be interpreted metaphorically. He describes people in certain physical conditions, and it is true, of course, that God can and does deliver us out of such physical conditions. But in addition to that, and over and above it, physical deliverances are but parables and signposts pointing to what God does for us in an infinitely bigger manner in a spiritual sense and with respect to our souls.

Now I have indicated that it is very generally agreed that this is probably a psalm which has reference to the captivity of the children of Israel. So all his pictures and illustrations can be thought of primarily in terms of the deliverance of the children of Israel from that actual captivity. But that, in turn, is nothing but a great picture of the deliverance which our souls have in Christ, in a spiritual sense, out of our spiritual bondage and captivity.

We say, then, that they are all to be interpreted mainly in that metaphorical sense, and we shall do so now with this first illustration. Another important point to bear in mind as we approach these examples is that undoubtedly each one of them is meant to be a picture of sin. Sin is a small word but it is very powerful, and sin is something that manifests itself in an almost endless variety of ways. That is a part of its subtlety, of course, and it is because we fail to realise this that we sometimes do not recognise it even when we are looking at it. We tend to think that sin always appears in the same way, but it does not. Most people can recognise sin when it appears in rags, but many do not recognise it when it appears in evening dress! Many people can recognise sin as it may manifest itself in the slum area of a great city, but they do not recognise it in the more affluent areas. Yet it is the same thing.

To use an illustration, sin is a disease that has many symptoms, and the object of the Psalmist is to give us some examples of these. He shows us in every case how they have the same source: it is sin at the root. But his point is that whatever the manifestation of the disease, God can heal it and deliver us from it. In every case he says, 'Then they cried unto the LORD in their trouble', and every time he goes on to say, 'and he delivered them out of their distresses' (v.6).

So it does not matter what form sin may take; if we but cry unto the Lord he will deliver us. Let us now consider that as it is proved and illustrated by this first picture which he gives us in verses 4-9. Here, obviously, we are looking at sin in terms of that which causes us to lose our way. One of the right etymological definitions of sin is *missing the mark*. A man is aiming at a target, but sin comes in and the bullet is deflected and he does not hit the bull's eye. Missing the mark; missing the way; not reaching the objective; stepping aside; being side-tracked. And this first illustration gives us a most extraordinarily vivid and dramatic picture of sin, as that which causes us to lose ourselves in life and in this world, and to miss the goal for which we were destined and intended.

Picture One—Losing our Way

So let us first look at the picture together, and then let us draw a few principles of teaching from it. This is a very common picture of sin in the Scriptures; you will find it in many places. What is the sort of person that we are dealing with here? Listen to the description: 'They wandered in the wilderness in a solitary way; they found no city to dwell in. Hungry and thirsty, their soul fainted in them. Then they cried unto the LORD in their trouble, and he delivered them out of their distresses.' Now here we are looking at the so-called intellectual type of person. The picture is of people in a wilderness, a desert, who are trying to find a city of habitation. They are looking for a city in which they can dwell and in which they can obtain certain satisfactions. But the trouble is that they cannot find it. They are in this wilderness which is a trackless waste; there are no paths there that lead them to the city. They are going backwards and forwards, looking, seeking; in a sense it is the whole picture of the human race from the very dawn of history. Mankind is looking for a city.

Quest for truth

But, in particular, we are concerned with this as it is depicted here in the *intellectual sense.* It is a picture, if you like, of people who are out in the great search and quest for truth. It is a picture of men and women seeking for intellectual understanding and satisfaction. They find themselves in this life and in this world, yes, but they have been given certain gifts. They have a mind and it begins to become active and they begin to ask questions. That is excellent. It is how it should be. And the great questions they ask themselves are these: What is life? Where has it all begun? Where has the world come from? Has it always existed or did it come into being at a given point? What is this extraordinary elusive thing we call life? You look at an animal and it is full of life, bounding, active; suddenly you see that animal dead and lifeless. The body is there but the life has gone. It is the same with a flower. And it is the same with man himself. What is life?

Now any thoughtful person, any person with a brain and who

really uses it, is bound to face these questions. These are the people we are looking at here; this intellectual type of person that is out for an understanding of life, its meaning, its purpose. That is the city. The city of intellectual rest, of intellectual satisfaction. It is the search—and it is as old as humanity—for a whole philosophy of life, for a complete view of existence including, especially, man himself. If you like it in more technical terms, it is a search for a philosophy of life, for a way of life, for an outlook that really will be satisfactory.

You simply have to read the story of mankind and you will find that this has been prominent; the intellectual activity of men and women has been tremendous. They have been facing the mystery of life. You will find it in ancient writings; you will find it even in mythology. People are looking for some philosopher's stone, some crystal, or something into which they can look and solve the riddle of existence and of the universe. They are looking for the city, the city of truth. They are not only seeking intellectual satisfaction; they are also seeking for *rules for living*, because living is a problem—human relationships; how to get on with other people, and so on. Men and women are ever seeking for these rules; seeking, in other words, for some kind of code or instruction which will enable them to do these things without constantly being immersed and overwhelmed in problems, and being upset and cast down and frustrated. They have always been looking for some kind of prescription, some law that can be dictated, which will suddenly put all these things right. People are doing it as busily and as actively today as they have ever done. That is the type of person we are looking at.

But not only that; it continues and includes something further. As we go on in life, we are ever aware of certain problems and difficulties which arise. There are certain riddles in life. We see things over and above our intellectual quest and the intellectual restlessness that asks for satisfaction and solutions. Over and above that, and even as we are engaged in that, things happen to us; and men and women have been battling with this problem too from the very beginning. O 'the slings and arrows of outrageous fortune'! O the buffetings and bludgeonings of chance! That is the problem.

But what can we do about these? Especially, how can we understand them? Why do these things happen to us? Why do things go wrong? Why is there illness? Why is there pestilence? Why are there storms? Why are there calamities? Why are there wars? Those are the questions. They come and hit us in life, and all along we have been seeking to understand them. Is there a purpose in it all, or is there not? Is life but a chessboard, and are we but the pieces upon it that are being manipulated helplessly by some unseen forces? Is it possible to reduce this total experience of ours in this life and world to some ordered reason? Can I discover the philosopher's stone—the answer to all these questionings?

Now we are looking at the kind of people who are concerned about all this, and there is one final thing I want to say about them. They are also searching for *security* and for *protection*. That is universally true, is it not? It has never been more obvious perhaps than it is today. Security is the great word: we are all making pacts, and the countries are making pacts; and the tragedy of life is that it is in our desire for security that we provoke war. But it is security we are out for. The nations on the other side of the Iron Curtain assure the world that they want nothing but security. They feel that they are being menaced and attacked. And the other half of the world is saying exactly the same thing. We want security, and we want it in an individual and in a personal sense also. There are things that are always threatening us: illness, accident, old age, and death itself always standing in the background, and ever coming nearer and nearer to us.

But, throughout their long existence in this world, men and women have been crying out for this security: some protection, some tower of safety into which they can go in the evil day that is bound to come; a place where they will be protected against it all and be able to recline in peace. That is the quest. Like the people in the psalm, they are seeking for a city to dwell in, 'a city of habitation'.

Now the Psalmist puts it to us, you remember, in his thoroughly dramatic manner, but what he really tells us about these people is that they clearly are not able to find the path. It is a wilderness, a trackless waste; they find no city to dwell in. So I want to consider this whole problem with you, this whole picture. You do not need much imagination to see it, do you? Many of us have known it, perhaps from personal experience.

Failure

We start out in this quest when we are young, and at first it is really most thrilling and most exciting. We start off with the assured conviction that where everybody has failed before us, we will succeed. And every generation thinks the same thing! Every generation is proud of itself and always despises the previous ones. 'Ah yes! They didn't know; they hadn't advanced; they hadn't the knowledge that we have; but, after all, *we* are really going to do it.' That is very true today, is it not? So we start off like that, full of confidence, full of assurance, full of resilience. 'Of course', we say, 'we are going to arrive at the city! Of course we are going to get there!' To us, the quest itself is the thing. It is most enjoyable, and in this mood we rather tend to smile at older people. 'To travel hopefully is better than to arrive,' we say. The exercise of our great brain! We do not want to arrive, it is just this great intellectual exercise; it is so exciting!

Doing the rounds

So we rush into the wilderness and we are going to get a straight run through to the city of habitation. There is the enjoyment of travelling, the intellectual curiosity. 'We want to read all sides,' we say; our minds are capacious enough to take it all in, so we try this

33

and we try that. We go the round of the philosophies, perhaps the round of the religions. Why? Well, we are interested in truth. We are really not selfish, we are not personal, we are not talking about being 'saved' or anything like that. We just want to give a little scope to these great minds of ours, and we want to garner knowledge and information from every direction.

So off we go with this thrilling enjoyment of the amazing quest for truth. And, of course, as we enter into this wilderness to seek for this highway, we meet certain people who offer to guide us. They are very ready to do so; they are very glad to meet somebody who really has a brain and who is intellectually alive and alert, and who is able to laugh at the past and all that has been taught hitherto. They are so delighted to meet us, and they say, 'Of course, you just follow me and listen to me and read my books and follow my lectures, and I will bring you to the city of habitation.' So we go after them, but we do not seem to arrive.

And then we meet another who tells us that, of course, that idea was quite wrong, it is out of date now. No, it is *this*; this is the latest. Again we find the same charm and we go with the same eagerness, but again we do not arrive.

Oh, I am not romancing, I am simply describing to you what so many people in this world are doing at this very moment. They are going the rounds of the philosophers, the round of the teachers, the round of the cults, the round of all these things that are being offered to us as the solution of the problems of mankind. But we do not seem to arrive at the city, and after a while we discover that the very guides whom we have trusted do not know where they are themselves. They have not arrived either. We may first of all, perhaps, discover it in their way of living and in their idea of morals, but, at any rate, we discover that they do not arrive in any sense at all. We thought they were so wonderful, but they do not know the way. They are false guides; they have raised false hopes within us.

Disillusioned

Then, when we have done a round of so many of them, at last we begin to wonder. We begin to feel that time is passing, that we are getting older and we are still very much where we were at the beginning. We have read so many books; we have listened to so many lectures; we have followed so many men; but actually when we face ourselves and our life and our understanding and death and eternity, we just have to admit that we are exactly where we were at the beginning. We do not know any more. We have not advanced a single step. We have been walking, we have been travelling certainly, and we thought we had struck many a pathway that looked as if it was going to lead to a highway—but it did not! We are back again in a trackless waste. We have gone round and round in circles.

But, unfortunately, it does not stop even at that. Life goes on, and it is no longer early morning with a bright shining sun. Noonday has passed, teatime has gone, the shadows of the night begin to appear, there is an ominous mist in the distance, and we still do not have a track. We are not on any way that gives us any assurance of bringing us to a city. And not only that, we begin to feel tired; we have walked so much; we have struggled so much; there was some brushwood we had to get out of the way in certain paths. We were told that effort was needed, and we made it; and we have tired ourselves and we are beginning to feel hungry: 'Hungry and thirsty, their soul fainted in them.'

You see, we have passed middle age now. We are beginning to get old and the night is coming on and the shadows are lengthening; our powers are feebler, and when somebody comes and says, 'I have a book: you read this. It will . . .', we say, 'I am sorry. I have read so many. I have been told it so often. Please don't bother me.' We have not got the energy to read any more books or to argue any longer. It was marvellous fifty and sixty years ago, but we cannot do it any longer. 'Hungry and thirsty', our souls are melting, as it were, within us. 'Their soul fainted in them,' says the Psalmist.

And here we are, drawing ever nearer and nearer to the end, distressed and, at last, feeling even desperate. At the end of a long life we are exactly where we were at the beginning, only that we are no longer young and we have lost our resilience and our capacity to recover. We have lost faith and hope; we have lost elasticity, we are failing, we are going down and we are drooping; we are hungry and we are thirsty; our knees are tottering, and the end is coming and the night is falling; we are going out of the world and we do not know where.

'Then they cried unto the LORD in their trouble.' And then an amazing statement: 'and he delivered them out of their distresses'. You know, I am almost tempted to pronounce the benediction at this point because that is the whole story, the whole gospel. It is just that!

But there may be someone who feels, 'Yes, that is a marvellous picture, but is it true? What are you really teaching? What are you saying?' Well, I have given it as a picture; let me now put it in the form of principles, propositions. Here is the first: the teaching of the Bible from beginning to end is that there is no way in life and there is no truth about life apart from the Lord Jesus Christ. So, as we consider this picture in Psalm 107:4-9, let us also bear in mind John 14:6. 'They wandered in the wilderness in a solitary way; they found no city to dwell in.'—'I am the way, the truth, and the life: no man cometh unto the Father, but by me.'

The answer

That is the answer, but let me work it out with you. There it is as a bald proposition. There is no way, no truth in this world apart from Christ. Now that is not a dogmatic assertion. That is something that I can prove to you, and I can do so out of the mouths of people who do not believe the Bible. I can prove it to you out of the mouths of humanists. That is the popular word today, is it not? Scientific humanism, I am told, is *the* thing, the thing that will really bring me to 'the city of habitation'.

Not humanism

So then, when I am told that, I always go to the best and to the high-est authorities I can find. I do not know of any greater scientific humanist in this country today, or perhaps in the world, than Dr Julian Huxley. And what does he tell us? Well, he tells us that his studies and his researches have brought him to the conclusion that there is no design, no meaning, no purpose, and no end in life. It is all accidental. It is all a matter of chance. You never know what will happen next. There are what he calls 'spots', biological spots, which means that certain things are thrown up now and again, nobody knows why or how. There is no sense, no rhyme, no reason in it; it just happens. He says that there is no purpose in creation, no purpose in life whatsoever. You cannot predict, you cannot prophesy the future. You cannot tell whether mankind is going up or going down. It may appear to be going up, and then the whole thing may suddenly be smashed. There is nothing in it. He does not know. Is that the way to come to the city of habitation? That is the voice of *scientific humanism* speaking.

But let us turn for a moment to the voice of *classical humanism*. This teaches that, after all, the key to life and the understanding of life is to be found in the teaching of the great philosophers of the past, starting with the great Greek pagan philosophers, none of whom were Christians, of course, and most of their followers have not been either. But that is the meaning of classical humanism: you go back and study this accumulated wisdom of the ages and of the centuries, the great literature of the world, and as you do so you will be given the wisdom that you need in life and in this world. Follow that, we are told.

So let us again go to the greatest authority of all in this connec-tion, and that is none other than Professor Gilbert Murray of Oxford, who is not a Christian and says so. A great man, a great brain, a great classical scholar and philosopher, but what does he tell us? Well, he was honest enough to admit that the last war [the

Second World War] had shaken him. He did not understand mankind; he did not understand why, but he saw clearly that mankind was not applying this classical knowledge. And so what has he to offer us? He still tells us to go back to something that has been there so long but which is not leading people to this satisfaction. It fails. Then, coming greatly down the scale, if you want popular exponents of these views, no man ever said more for the kind of thing I am describing than the late H. G. Wells. But do you remember his very last book of all? He gave it this significant title, *Mind at the End of its Tether.* He did not know where he was. The man who had preached so much throughout his life and who said he *knew*, ends by saying he does not know. And he did not!

I shall not weary you with exact quotations, but if you do not take my word for it, then, at the risk of being misunderstood, I advise you to read these men and you will find this. I think that the most horrible description of humanity and of life that I ever read was a description of life by Bertrand Russell who, again, is utterly hopeless about it all; hopeless about the present and much more hopeless about the future. He sees nothing there at all except blackness and darkness engulfing us. And the only thing he can be pleased about is that he believes that when we do go out of this world, that is the end of it all. It is just ceasing to exist, and in a sense he almost thanks God that that is what is going to happen; but he does not believe in God, so he does not thank him. But it is sheer hopelessness, it is final despair. They do not know—these greatest leaders and writers—they are baffled, they are bewildered, they do not know and they do not understand. And, let me say this for them, they are honest enough to say so.

No hope
But as there is no way and no truth apart from Christ, there is no life apart from him either. 'Hungry and thirsty, their soul fainted in them.' Yes, but when you come to Christ, you read this: 'he

38

satisfieth the longing soul, and filleth the hungry soul with goodness' (v.9).

There is no satisfaction apart from him; there is no hope apart
from him. Again I am not simply making dogmatic assertions. I can
prove it, and if you want my proof, I simply tell you to read the
autobiographies and biographies of great men who have not been
Christians. Quite a number have been written recently and I know
of nothing more hopeless.

I hope you do not misunderstand me. There was a great man
called Lord Simon who was once the Lord Chancellor of England.
He wrote his autobiography not long before he died. Read it if you
want to see the hopelessness of a man who trusts only to intellect
and who does not believe in God and who does not know the Lord
Jesus Christ. Poor man! He is trying to be happy by looking back
at his great legal successes and the heyday of his life. Now I am not
criticising these men, I am simply giving facts and I am simply saying that I am sorry for them. They do not know, and at the end they
go out into blackness and darkness and despair.

Do you know the end of the life story of Charles Darwin?
Charles Darwin turned his back upon God and a belief in God, and
gave himself to pure scientific research, because he believed that
therein he would find the problem solved and the solution to all
these difficulties. But, poor Darwin!—this is in his official biography—at the end of his life he found that he had lost his appreciation for poetry, for music, and even for a glorious landscape. Oh,
what a narrowing of the soul, what a fettering of a life, what an
atrophy of faculties! A man who used to enjoy poetry and music
and the glories of nature and of creation, he lost his appreciation.
His soul had shrivelled, it had dwindled into nothing.

But shall I summarise it by putting it in some words that I am
fond of quoting, because they often seem to me to be the perfect
expression of the hopelessness of life without Christ? They are the
words of Walter Savage Landor:

> *I strove with none; for none was worth my strife;*

You see the cynic?

> *Nature I loved, and, next to Nature, Art;*

You see the intellectual? He loves nature and he loves art, sculpture, paintings, music, literature, anything that is artistic, and he had had a marvellous time. He had lived this full intellectual life.

> *I warmed both hands before the fire of life;*

—and oh, how enjoyable and warm and enriching it was!

> *It sinks . . .*

While I am looking at it the fire is going out, the fuel is ended. I have coaxed it, I have blown it, it is going out, it sinks. And what about it?

> *. . . and I am ready to depart.*

There is nothing left, it is going, it is leaving me. I am left alone and I can do nothing about it. I have nothing to look forward to, I am going out, there is the end.

Life without Christ is utterly hopeless. There is no way, no path, no life, no truth. It is a wilderness, a solitary way, and it leaves us helpless and hopeless and lost; hungry and thirsty, and with our souls fainting within us.

But, my dear friends, there is no need to go out like that. 'They cried unto the LORD in their trouble, and he delivered them out of their distresses.' Listen! 'He led them forth by the right way, that they might go to a city of habitation.' That's it! And 'He satisfieth the longing soul and filleth the hungry soul with goodness.' Christ is 'the way, the truth, and the life'.

'Ah, but', you say,' we no longer believe in that: that is in the realm of folklore.' But is it not amazing that anybody should still go on saying that? The newspapers must be tragically short of news to go on repeating something that has been said so often. Any fool in a bar parlour in London tonight is saying that; he has always said it. There is nothing new in saying that there is no God and that Christ is a myth. I remember a poor old man being converted at the age of 77, and his greatest trouble in his life from there on was that thirty years before in a drunken argument and brawl he had said, 'Jesus Christ is a bastard.' He was not given press publicity for saying that, but he said what is always being said.

I confess I do not quite understand the mentality of this modern world we are living in. I read a psalm in the Old Testament which says, 'The fool hath said in his heart, There is no God' (Psalm 14:1; Psalm 53:1). Have we advanced beyond that? Of course we have not! It is simply a dogmatic assertion with no proof whatsoever. It is simply repeating things which cannot be proved in any way at all. It does not take into consideration for a moment the order, the arrangement, in the cosmos. It does not take into account human history. It does not take into account the fact of Jesus Christ.

What I do not quite understand about these people is why they speak of 1955 if they really believe what they say. Why do they call it 1955? Why do they adopt that chronology? If you are to be scientific, you must not do that sort of thing. If you do not believe that Christ has ever lived, why do you speak of 1955? It is rubbish; it is nonsense; you are dwelling on a folklore, you are repeating it day by day, and it is very wrong of you to tell your children that this is 16 January 1955. You must not tell them fables and fairy tales.

I almost apologise for having said all that. Oh, it is pathetic, it is tragic! Shall I say something else that may surprise you much more? The people who do harm to Christianity are not those people; we do not expect anything better from them. The fool will go on saying in his heart, 'There is no God' (Psalm 14:1). 'The world by wisdom knew not God' (1 Corinthians 1:21). The Bible has prepared us for all this. It says that the 'natural man' cannot know him—do not expect him to and do not be surprised when he

does not. Such people do not do any harm. I do not expect un-
believers to glory in the Lord Jesus Christ; they have never seen
him; they do not know him; they are blinded by 'the god of this
world' (2 Corinthians 4:4). That does not trouble me at all. The real
harm is done by people who call themselves Christians and who are
members, and sometimes ministers, in the Christian Church, but
who deny the miraculous and the virgin birth and the supernatural.
They are the people that do the harm.

The right way

So Christ is the answer. He is the way. Yes, he leads them by the
right way, which means a straight way. Thank God, it is a way
which is direct and simple. This is how the Old Testament puts it:
the way to truth that Christ has opened is a way of which it can be
said that 'the wayfaring men, though fools, shall not err therein'
(Isaiah 35:8). As Paul puts it, 'not many wise . . . not many noble,
are called' (1 Corinthians 1:26). Thank God!

Here is a way that brings me to the city of truth, and I do not
need to be a philosopher. I do not need to have been through the
universities; because, if that is the way, then those people who have
not had a secondary and a university education are doomed and
damned. But here is a way that anybody can walk through. Why?
Because it means following a person. It is a simple way, a direct
way. It is a way for 'fools'. It is a way for ignoramuses. It is a way
for people who have failed, for people whose very brain has
become befuddled by drink and vice. It is a way that is prepared by
God inside us and outside us. It is a direct way, a straight way, a
simple way. It is God's way. 'Christ is the way, the truth, and the
life.'

The gospel is so gloriously simple and direct, and it tells us at
once that there is only one question that we need consider. You
need not read all these great books on philosophy, because there is
only one problem and that is the relationship of men and women to

God. It goes straight to the centre. It says that this is the only problem in all people. Whether you are an intellectual or whether you are as dull as a person can be, it does not matter, it is the same problem—you are not rightly related to God and your life will not be right until God begins to bless you. The need, the quest, is only that of knowing God and getting to him. 'Thou hast made us for thyself', said one of the greatest philosophers of all, Augustine (afterwards of Hippo). He tried philosophy, but while he was a philosopher he was immoral and kept his mistress; though he did not know it, he was in the wilderness. But at last he saw it: 'Thou hast made us for thyself, and our souls are restless until they find their rest in thee.' He found it; and he found it in Jesus Christ.

Jesus Christ, the Son of God, came into this world in order to make a way from man to God. He came into the wilderness, he charted it and mapped out a road, and he made it. How do you know he has made it? Well, this is how he has made a road: he has put his own body down and we step over him. He laid down his life, his body; it was broken and his blood was shed; the bread and the wine remind us of this, and we, as it were, walk over his broken body and his shed blood. It is a glorious highway, and it brings us to God.

In all our need and helplessness and failure, we come to him and see him and the truth as it is in him. We find that we are brought to God, and God takes hold of us and gives us a new life and a new nature and everything we need. It is the right way; it is a straight way.

A satisfying way

And, finally, it is a satisfactory way. 'He satisfieth the longing soul, and filleth the hungry soul with goodness' (v.9). He gives us complete satisfaction. Yes, intellectual satisfaction. I know of no problem but that the Bible gives me an answer to it. I mean what I say. I find complete intellectual satisfaction here, and whatever aspect of life you are concerned about, I can demonstrate it to you. A new view of life, a new outlook, a new explanation of my origin and beginning, and that of the world, an understanding of time; it is all here, humanity, sin, failure, all explained. Morally it gives me satisfaction: my sins forgiven; strength and guidance and power; the operation of the Holy Spirit within me; a new view of sin, and a new desire after holiness placed within me. And whatever circumstances and situations I may find myself in, it helps me to understand them and to explain them. 'All things work together for good to them that love God . . .' (Romans 8:28). All things! I understand illness in a new way. I understand disappointment in a new way. I understand death in a new way. Everything is made new: 'old things are passed away; behold, all things are become new' (2 Corinthians 5:17).

> *All the way my Saviour leads me,*
>   *What have I to ask beside?*
> *Can I doubt His tender mercy,*
>   *Who through life has been my guide?*
> *Heavenly peace, divinest comfort,*
>   *Here by faith in Him to dwell!*
> *For I know whate'er befall me,*
>   *Jesus doeth all things well.*

Frances Jane Van Alstyne

Where are you, my friend? That is the question. Have you been merely a listener as I have been speaking? A mere spectator? Or have you realised that I have been speaking about you? Where are you? Are you still in that wilderness, wandering backwards and forwards, seeking, trying, hoping, longing? Are the shadows beginning to lengthen? Do you know something of the despair and the hopelessness? If you do, I am privileged to say just this to you: cry out unto the Lord in your trouble. And, as certainly as you do so, he will deliver you out of your distresses.

I am happy to say this also. If you are young, then take it from me now; do not waste your time; you will end where you began. Turn to him *now*. You may have already felt the despair, because despair is not confined to old age. Young people can break their hearts—and they do. Turn to him now, therefore.

Yes, but I am equally glad to say this. It is not only for young people. You may have one foot in the grave, it does not matter. If you realise you are lost, cry out to him in your trouble even now, and he will assure you that though you have wasted valuable, precious years, and though you have denied him and mocked him and laughed at him and scoffed at him, and though you may have been guilty of every sin known to man, and are bespattered and besmirched and fouled by the mire of this world, he will not refuse you. He will listen to you. He will receive you now, and he will tell you that he sent his Son into the world to die for you and your sins; that he, therefore, forgives you in him, and will take you unto himself and make you his child and lead you into his own glorious presence.

So turn to him, even now.

3
The prison

*'Such as sit in darkness and in the shadow of
death, being bound in affliction and iron; because they
rebelled against the words of God, and contemned the
counsel of the most High: therefore he brought down their
heart with labour; they fell down, and there was none to help.
Then they cried unto the LORD in their trouble, and he saved them
out of their distresses. He brought them out of darkness and the
shadow of death, and brake their bands in sunder. Oh that men
would praise the LORD for his goodness, and for his wonderful
works to the children of men! For he hath broken the gates
of brass, and cut the bars of iron in sunder.'*
(Psalm 107:10-16)

The Psalmist's contention here, let me remind you, is that sin is something which can take many forms, but that though the forms vary, sin is still sin. There is a common origin, a common root to all the varied problems and ills of mankind, and the real trouble with mankind is that it does not realise that. Because it does not trace this common source, it tends to think that different types of people have different needs and different problems. But the fact is that 'One touch of nature makes the whole world kin' and that, according to the Scriptures, we are all under a common denominator because we have all sinned against God. That is the Psalmist's contention, and he proves it by giving us these illustrations. 'Here are four different symptoms', he seems to say. 'Yes, but there is only one essential disease.'

We have looked at his first picture, that of a number of people travelling about in a wilderness looking for a city of habitation in which to dwell. They could not find it; they became hungry and thirsty and tired and weary, and they did not know what to do. So in their distress they cried out unto the Lord and he heard them and delivered them. He brought them to a city to dwell in, and he fed them and gave them all they needed. That, I suggested, was a picture of sin as missing the mark. Sin is that which blinds our eyes and leads us astray.

That was a wonderful picture, but now we come to an entirely different one. And yet I want to emphasise that though the picture, on the surface, is so different, we shall find that the same principles are here. The troubles come out of the same common source and the same common origin. This is a vital principle.

Picture 2—Imprisoned

We are still looking at sin, but this time we are looking at it not as it leads us astray, nor as it causes us to miss the mark. We look here at sin as slavery, sin as that which leads to serfdom and to a state of terrible bondage.

Here, of course, is something, again, that is of great importance at this present time. In every one of these pictures we shall find the subtlety of sin coming out. For if there is one thing that characterises the devil, our great opponent and antagonist, more than anything else, it is subtlety. We are told that it was by his subtlety he deceived Eve (2 Corinthians 11:3) and, there is no question about it, he has continued to be subtle ever since. And here we have a perfect illustration of that. The common idea is that religion is something which fetters us and makes slaves of us, and that when you give up religion and become a 'man of the world' and a sort of humanist, then you are setting yourself at liberty. How often have we heard people saying that! 'Ah yes,' they say, 'of course, when I was a child I had to go to Sunday School and to Chapel, and so on; and as long as I was at home and under the authority and influence of my father and mother I had to do it. But when I left home I soon got rid of that. I threw it off!' They emancipated themselves; they stretched out their wings; they became free at last, and began to live truly. Religion? Some kind of incubus, something that hems us in and holds us down; but after religion, then great freedom and liberty.

That, I suppose, is the devil's masterpiece. He persuades us to think that by turning our backs upon God and by listening to him instead, we really are going to improve our lot and condition, and especially in terms of freedom. Of course, he did that, as the Bible tells us, at the very beginning. His whole suggestion to Eve, and through her to Adam, was that God was putting restrictions upon them; that he was not fair to them; that he was keeping something from them; that they were meant to be like gods themselves; and why should they not be? If they wanted truly to live and to express themselves, there was only one thing to do, and that was to defy God and really live as they should. It was the original temptation, and it has continued right down until now.

The devil is deluding men and women today in exactly the same way. He says that he is offering them freedom, liberty, emancipation, a large outlook, a great life to live. So different from the narrow, cramped, confined religious life! But that is the very stratagem with which the devil masters us and conquers us, places us in his own dominion and tyrannises over us and makes slaves of us.

Now that is the picture that is unfolded in these verses 10 to 16 in this section of Psalm 107. We are looking at a number of people sitting in prison cells: 'Such as sit in darkness and in the shadow of death, being bound in affliction and iron.' The man who wrote this psalm was a very great artist, apart from anything else, a very great poet, and a master painter with words. His theme, his case, is that though men and women may appear to be so absolutely different, they are really all one, and they are one in the same condition.

Now look how he does this. He gives us as his second picture one that seems to be a contrast in every single respect to his first picture. The first, as I have reminded you, was a picture of men wandering about in a wilderness. The trouble with them, in a sense, was that the place was too big and that they could not narrow it down to a pathway that would lead them to the city. But here we are looking at people in a cell, in a narrow confined space, whose feet are fast in the stocks; they are bound in irons, they cannot move at all. If the trouble before was too much room, the trouble now is not enough room. If the trouble before was that they were wandering about and walking until they were tired out, the trouble is now that they cannot walk, they are not allowed to move. It seems to be a complete contrast, and one's first reaction is to say that surely there can be nothing whatsoever in common between these two groups of people.

But wait a minute! Let us go on and follow his description and his delineation of these people in detail, because it is such a perfect picture of life. I am free to confess that I find it very difficult to understand an intelligent person who does not see, were it merely from this passage, that this book must be the Word of God. Can you not see how well it knows us? Can you not see how well it knows life? Can you not see the accuracy of its psychological knowledge? It is not a book that merely makes statements; it gives us these detailed descriptions and, as you read them, you see that really the man is describing us ourselves. He is describing men and women and life as it is today. We are all interested in psychology and in reading books about it. We say, 'During these last hundred years, we have acquired a very great and profound knowledge of human nature and the secrets and the sources of human action and behaviour. It is only with this analysis of ours that we have really discovered it.'

Stuff and nonsense!—forgive the expression!—it is all here. This Psalmist knew all about it. I defy you to give me a more profound psychological analysis of human nature and the sources of behaviour than you will find in the Scriptures. It is all here with a depth and a profundity that no one else can contend. Follow it! He says that they are sitting in darkness. They are in dungeons, not only in darkness but in 'the shadow of death'. That is his way of describing gloom, and a very intense gloom; it is a very profound sort of obscurity. You know the sort of prisons they had in the old days before prison reform came in: they were generally underground; they were dark, and they were damp and dank. That is what he is describing, and you notice the vivid way in which he brings out the darkness and the gloom and the obscurity of it all. In the prison cell. Down in the depths somewhere. You can visit old castles and sometimes you can see these dungeons in which they kept the prisoners. That will give you an idea of what this man has in his mind in his description.

But he does not stop at that. Not only are these people in this kind of cell, he also tells us that they are 'bound in affliction and iron'. He means that they are in a state of terrible affliction because they are bound with irons; their feet have iron bands upon them, and these, in turn, are connected with chains which are fixed into the wall; and, conceivably, there are handcuffs upon them and they may even be joined to the wall. The cruelty of this kind of imprisonment is indeed most astonishing.

That is his general description of them. They are wretched and unhappy in such an awful plight and condition. But he goes on to tell us that all this is but a part of a great prison, because you notice that, later on, he talks about bars of iron and gates of brass. It is a picture of a great prison-house. As you approach this prison you see that there are great walls right round it; then you come up to the main entrance, and there are these mighty gates of brass or of bronze; and, as you go inside, you see that the most elaborate precautions have been taken. There are iron bars even covering doors. There are slits which are supposed to let in a certain amount of air and light and ventilation, but there are iron bars there. Nobody can ever get out through them. And if a man should succeed almost by some miracle in getting out of his cell, he will soon come up against some obstruction, some kind of iron bars again, and some kind of door and a gate. That is the picture of a prison, and these people are all inmates of such a prison. It is a picture, in other words, of complete helplessness. You cannot imagine a more accurate description of a condition of complete serfdom and slavery, and it is a condition in which men and women are entirely hopeless.

But then he tells us that in this utter hopelessness they 'cried unto the LORD in their trouble, and he saved them out of their distresses'. So what does all this represent? What is the Psalmist concerned to say to us? Let me put it to you like this. What has brought these people to such a state? Why is it that any men or women should ever arrive at this condition? Well, he has already given us the answer. He tells us that it is entirely their own fault. It is as a consequence of their own deliberate actions that they are where they are and as they are, and they can do nothing whatsoever about it.

But, thank God, he does not stop at that. He starts with this picture of complete hopelessness and then he opens the door of everlasting and eternal hope. His message is that in spite of their condition, and the fact that they richly deserve to be where and what they are, these people, when they cry out unto the Lord, are heard of him, and he delivers them out of all their distresses and troubles and sets them at liberty.

The message

There, then, is the picture, but what is the message? Let me summarise it like this. It is the message concerning sin and its consequences, the only way and the only hope of deliverance from which is by the grace of God. Let me show this to you in terms of a number of principles. Here is the first. What is sin? 'You go on talking about sin,' says someone, 'but what exactly is it?' The Psalmist's reply in the eleventh verse is this. He says that these people 'sit in darkness and in the shadow of death, being bound in affliction and iron; *because they rebelled against the words of God, and contemned the counsel of the most High.*'

Rebellion

And the answer of the Bible everywhere is in the same terms as it is here. Sin is rebellion against God and against God's words. You will never discover a more profound definition of sin than that. A sinner is a man or woman who is a rebel against God, a rebel against God's will, a rebel against God's law. So we must start with this biblical definition of sin and of a sinner, otherwise we shall not be able to follow the message. So often people think of sin in terms of *sins*, and when you ask them to define sin, they say, 'Well, sin, of course, is doing something which isn't nice, something which isn't good.' Or they may put it positively by saying that sin is doing something that is wrong; it is an unworthy action, a deed that is prohibited. But their definition stops at that, and they have not mentioned God. And that is why certain nice, respectable people think that they are not sinners at all because they have never done those things. But once you begin to see that sin is to be defined in terms of our relationship to God, then you find that everybody is a sinner, because the essence of sin is to rebel against God and against God's holy law.

Sin, in other words, is to put my will instead of God's will, my idea instead of God's idea. Sin, if you like, can be described as the failure to glorify God with the whole of my being and in everything that I do. So, to forget God is to be a sinner. To do your own will and not God's will, though it may not involve some terrible open action, that is still sin. They rebelled against the words of God. Sin, in other words, is men and women setting up their own authority, and living as they think they ought to live, instead of doing what God tells them to do.

The second characteristic is that they 'contemned the counsel of the most High', which means that, with contempt, they spurned and rejected God's way and offer of deliverance. The essence of sin is all there in just that one verse. The whole trouble with men and women is just this twofold fact: that they do not bow their knees to God, and that they go even further than that; they reject with scorn the fact that God's action, which has been taken in order to deliver them out of their troubles, is salvation in his Son, our Lord and Saviour Jesus Christ. They 'contemn the counsel of the most High'. They ridicule Christ and his blood and his death and spit upon his great salvation. That is the Psalmist's definition of sin. He puts it in the form of a picture, but it is what the New Testament tells us about sin everywhere.

Arrogance and ignorance

Then let us notice a second thing about sin, which is its arrogance and its ignorance. Have you noticed, in this eleventh verse again, the way in which he puts it? He says they are in this condition because 'they rebelled against the words of God'. That is the translation in the Authorised [King James] version. But God has many different names, and if you read your Old Testament in the original language you will find that different names and different words are used which are translated here as *God*. And the word that is used here is this: they are in these conditions because they rebelled against the words of 'the Mighty One', the God who is might and strength and power, the mightiest of all.

And whose counsel is it that they have contemned? They have 'contemned the counsel of the most High'. The highest One. The One who is in the highest heavens; who is over all. That is why I speak about the ignorance and the unutterable arrogance of sin. If there is nothing else to be said about sin, we can say that it is the greatest folly of which men and women have ever been guilty. Go back again to the Garden of Eden and consider it there. Adam and Eve were living a life in communion with God. They knew that he

54

was God the Creator who had made everything out of nothing; the God who ordered and who controlled everything; and yet, what did they do? They rebelled against such a God. They were but human beings, creatures, made by God. He had fashioned them out of the very dust of the earth and had breathed into Adam the breath of life, and had formed the woman out of him. Adam knew God's might and his power, and yet, look at him! It was raving, stark madness and lunacy—he stood up against and rebelled against the Mighty One.

And that is precisely what men and women are still doing. They say in their ignorance, 'I don't believe there is a God.' Or they criticise him for doing this and for not doing that. And do you see what is happening? Pygmy creatures of time, such as we are, our very life is but a breath and as a vapour. We are here today and we are gone tomorrow. There are around us at this moment little germs that are so small that they will pass through the smallest and the most delicate filters. They are called ultramicroscopic filter-passing viruses. They are as weak and as small as that, and yet they can knock us down and kill us with pneumonia. Such is our feebleness.

And yet, what do we do? We rebel against the Mightiest. Oh, the folly, the ignorance and the arrogance of sin, that pygmy human beings should stand against God! We are in the hands of God, our very breath, our very life, is in God's hands, and yet people say, 'I don't care!' Like a feeble fly trying to resist the advance of a tractor or a steamroller! Multiply that by infinity and there is the picture. Men and women in their weakness, the creatures of a day, standing up against the eternal, the absolute, the almighty One. Ah yes, and spurning and dismissing with contempt the advice, the counsel, the proffered salvation of the Highest.

My dear friends, what fools we are! Sin is ignorance, it is appalling ignorance. It is because we do not realise what we are doing that we live as we do. It is because we do not realise exactly what our sin means and constitutes that we persist in it. It is un-utterable folly, and it is not surprising that the results which follow do so of necessity.

Results

Let me note them to you. That is what people do in sin; and they bring upon themselves, and are alone responsible for, the consequences of such behaviour. Here they are. Sin, of course, as I have been pointing out, because of the subtlety of the devil, seems wonderful at first; and people talk about their marvellous life and about 'seeing life'. How wonderful it is as you look at it in the newspapers and see the pictures; you buy these weekly picture-papers, and see the glamour and the romance, the glitter and the charm of it all.

Ah yes, and young people reading such things, and looking at them on the films and in other places, say, 'That is life; that is the thing I am after; that's what I want. What a life that is!' That was how the people in these verses in Psalm 107 once thought. But wait a minute! It does not, alas, stop at that. This is what you find: 'Therefore he brought down their heart with labour; they fell down, and there was none to help.' What is the Psalmist talking about? He is simply giving a description of life. Do not merely read the life of the men and women of the world in their early days; go on, read the full story, go through to the end. Follow them on, see what that kind of life really leads to, and you will find that it leads eventually to some form of hard labour. It is God, we are told, that brings down their heart with labour. The Bible puts that in another place in a very pregnant phrase: it says, 'the way of transgressors is hard' (Proverbs 13:15).

A hard life
The life of sin is a hard life. It is all very well to look at these glamorous pictures on the front pages of the journals, but before

you come to a conclusion about that sort of life, visit the lodging houses and the doss houses; visit the reformatories; visit the little rooms with scarcely any adornments upon the walls, and scarcely a bed in them worthy of the name. Look at the end of a life which began in apparent glamour and wonder and thrill.

If you read the story of mankind in the history books and bio-graphies and autobiographies, there is nothing that stands out more plainly than this: that the way of the transgressors is hard. It always becomes a hard labour. Difficulties and problems arise; things do not seem to continue as they did. I need not keep you about this; I apologise for stressing it as much as I do. The newspapers tell you perfectly well all that I am trying to say. You can spit upon the sanctities, you can laugh at your marriage vows and say, 'That is Victorianism, that is the Bible—I do not believe that sort of thing. I am really going in for something new and fresh, and this is going to be perfect.'

But is it perfect? Keep your eyes open and you will see the same people saying and doing exactly the same things all over again: 'he brought down their heart with labour'. And not only that, it gets even worse: 'they fell down, and there was none to help'. A better translation would be, *'they began to stumble'*. This, I believe, is the Psalmist's way of describing pictorially some of the complications that always arise in a life of sin. Nobody has ever yet sinned in this world without complications coming in. It was a marvellous thing, thought Adam and Eve, was it not, to listen to the devil and to stand up against God, to assert their rights and to eat the forbidden fruit. But the moment they did it, there was a problem: they heard the voice of God, and they said, 'What shall we do?' They had to cover themselves up somehow. You have to keep up pretences, and they vanish and disappear at once.

Look at Cain! He involved himself in terrible trouble the moment he murdered his brother, and you cannot enter on a life of sin before you begin to stumble. There are complications. Do what you will, you cannot avoid them. I am speaking to your experience. I am speaking my own experience. You have a conscience worrying you. You seem to have got out of one trouble but you are in another and, indeed, the old one is still there. There are difficulties; there are people who misunderstand you, and everything is not as perfect in the world as you thought it was; the other companion you may have chosen is not all that you thought, and so on. You begin to stumble. You are not walking as straight as you thought you were going to do; difficulties arise on all sides; you do not know where you are and you begin to fall. Stumbling!

Slavery

But it gets even worse! It leads to slavery and imprisonment, as I told you in my picture at the beginning: 'Such as sit in darkness and in the shadow of death, being bound in affliction and iron'. At first we all choose to sin, but a day comes, if we persist in that life, when we cannot help sinning. Every time you sin you weaken your resistance. Every time you sin you are commencing a habit, and we all know the power of habit—ingrained habits, long-continued habits, lust and passion. You want to stop, but you cannot. You are a victim, you are held. You would give the whole world if you could stop. You try this and that, and this remedy and the other, but where are you? You are still held, you are in the grip of the thing, you are in a vice, and you cannot shake it off. Many a man's career has been ruined by drink. He has tried to stop drinking, and his wife and children have tried to stop him. But they cannot. He is held, he is a victim. He is in the chains; he is in the irons.

Sin weakens our willpower to such a point that we have none left. Sin is slavery, and I shall not insult you by arguing with you about it. Every one of us at this moment knows the slavery of sin. It may be drink. It may be something moral—sexual if you like. It may be bad temper. It may be a hasty word that you can never control. It may be jealousy and spite, evil imaginations, and all these things. And there you are, you know you are the victim of them. You are in a prison. You are a slave, you are in bondage. And such persons talk about freedom and liberty! Oh, the deceit of the devil!

Darkness

But it does not even stop at that. Go on with this history of the 'Rake's progress', and this is what you come to: darkness and gloom. God willing, I shall have more to say about that aspect of it, but it is here and it is always present in sin. It is invariable. The poor sinner enters a state of darkness and of unutterable helplessness. Oh, the misery and the wretchedness of a life burnt out in sin, a soul squandered on iniquity; the refuse, the wreckage of a noble being created by God! And look at such poor persons if they reach old age: indeed it often happens to them in mid life and even before that. They do not have a glimmer of hope; they have no light from any direction. It is gloom and hopelessness. Indeed, it is the very shadow of death itself, and there is no hope at all. They have lost everything, and they look into the future and see nothing but blackness and darkness illuminated by flashes of hell; in the shadow of death with nothing to do about it and with no one to turn to. That is the last point I would emphasise: 'they fell down, and there was none to help'.

Do you remember the Lord Jesus Christ describing all that in the parable of the Prodigal Son? 'No man gave unto him' (Luke 15:16). The poor fellow had been so prodigal with his money while he had his pockets full of it. He entertained his friends and had his boon companions, and they said he was the best fellow in the world and there was nothing they would not do for him. But when the famine came they all forsook him; they forgot him; they left him to himself. 'No man gave unto him'—absolutely left on the scrap heap, the refuse of life. Sin always does it because it is essential selfishness. There was none to help him in his distress and in his agony and in his pain; he was utterly lost and forsaken.

That is what the Bible has to say about a life of sin. It tells you that if you are living that selfish, self-centred, godless, worldly life, that will be your story. If you rebel against God and reject his offer in Christ, that is what awaits you; nothing else and nothing less. It is indeed a final picture of hell. Hell anticipated in this world; hell realised in all its agony and its torment in the next.

Deliverance

But, thank God, there is a deliverance. These people, we are told, in spite of all that I have said about them, 'cried unto the Lord in their trouble, and he delivered them out of all their distresses' (v.6). Oh, what a gospel! And that is why God should be praised. It is not merely that he does what he does for us. The marvellous thing to me is that he is ever prepared to do it. Why should he listen to them? They have rebelled against him. They have treated him with derision and scorn. They have spurned his life divine. And yet, when they are down and out and alone, they cry out to him, and he hears them and delivers them out of their distresses, in his goodness and his everlasting mercy.

And listen to the way in which he gives the deliverance. I do want you to follow these steps. I shall merely mention them: work them out for yourself on your bended knees, and thank God for them. How wonderful these steps are!

Coming out of darkness

As you go *down* the scale in the picture of sin's slavery, in redemption you come *up* the scale, and the first thing is that you come out of the darkness and gloom. In the unutterable darkness and despair of realising that you are a sinner and that you have sinned against God, you feel that nothing can save you and that you have no right to pray. You feel that if you did pray, God could not possibly listen to you. Man cannot help you. You cannot help yourself. There is nothing to be done. You are overcome by hopelessness. What can I, a guilty sinner, do? I am undone, I am lost.

Suddenly, into the gloom there appears a flash of light. What is this? Well, listen to the apostle Paul expressing it: 'For God, who commanded the light to shine out of darkness, hath shined in our hearts, to give the light of the knowledge of the glory of God in the face of Jesus Christ' (2 Corinthians 4:6). This light is in the face of Jesus Christ, and it tells us that one mightier than the devil has entered into this life and into this world. Read the eleventh chapter of the Gospel according to St Luke. What is man in sin? He is a man in that prison, kept by that 'strong man armed' whose 'goods are in peace' (Luke 11:21), and he can do nothing about it. 'But when a stronger than he shall come upon him, and overcome him, he taketh from him all his armour wherein he trusted' (Luke 11:22) and sets at liberty his captives. That is the light that comes.

Let me put it like this. In your shame and guilt, in the unutterable loneliness when everybody, as it were, has forsaken you; with your conscience condemning you and hammering at you, and the law of God shouting at you, and the whole world leaving you to yourself and saying, 'You have made your bed, lie on it; you have spilt the milk, you cannot gather it again'— into the midst of all that there comes a blessed person with a face that is so pure that you can scarcely look into it. And he smiles at you, and he comes and takes his place beside you. He was called the 'friend of publicans and sinners' (Luke 7:34). He is one who comes to you and says to you, 'Peace, be still' (Mark 4:39).

He tells you, as you listen to him, that he has not only seen you and is sorry for you. He tells you something that you can scarcely believe and that breaks your heart. He tells you that he loves you! He tells you that, though he was in heaven, he saw you and he loved you, even while you were in your arrogance and pride and defiance, and as you were flouting God, blaspheming his name, and spitting upon his salvation. He tells you that even then he loved you, while you were an enemy and an alien; that he came down from heaven to earth; and not only that, he deliberately went to the cross on Calvary for you, to bear your sins, to die for you, that you might be delivered. 'He brought them out of darkness and the shadow of death.' With arms full wide open he comes and takes hold of us and assures us that he is come to redeem us.

Breaking out of bondage

But he does not stop at that. Let me go on with the description. 'He brought them out of darkness and the shadow of death, and brake their bands in sunder' (v.14). These iron fetters, he strips them off, he is so strong. In other words, he sets us free. He sets us free from the condemnation of the law, and from the fear of death and the grave. 'There is therefore now no condemnation to them which are in Christ Jesus' (Romans 8:1). Justified freely by his grace, I am set free from the bondage of the law. He has dealt with the guilt of my sin; he has borne its punishment, and I am free.

But he goes even beyond that, and I thank God for this. He also breaks the power of sin. He sets the prisoner free. 'He breaks the power of cancelled sin.' He answers my prayer when I ask him to save me from its guilt and power. That is the salvation. It is all here, you see. This is the New Testament gospel: the light, the person, the fetters broken, the condemnation removed, the man emancipated, set free within, a new power and a new life.

But even more than that, listen to this—the Psalmist reserves this until the very end. He goes on to say, 'Oh that men would praise the L<small>ORD</small> for his goodness, and for his wonderful works to the children of men!' Why? For he has 'broken the gates of brass, and cut the bars of iron in sunder'. That translation is too weak; what it really means is that he *shatters* the gates of brass. He shatters them and breaks in two all bars of iron. And this means that not only am I set free from the power of sin within me, but I am delivered and emancipated from the power of sin outside me, as it is to be found in the world and the flesh and the devil. 'Sin shall not have dominion over you' (Romans 6:14). Satan has been mastered. The strong man armed has been taken. He has met his match and more. Christ has defeated him. Not only sin in me, but sin in the devil is mastered. He has met his Lord. He is in chains. He is held at bay. And, finally, he will be destroyed completely.

What is a Christian? Paul, in writing to the Colossians, says that he or she is one who has been 'delivered from the power of darkness and . . . translated into the kingdom of [God's] dear Son' (Colossians 1:13). You are taken out of the dominion of the devil and put into the dominion of Christ. You are surrounded by the walls of Christ's salvation and defence and are no longer in that terrible prison with the bars of iron and the gates of brass. He sets the prisoner free. Not only does he give me a new hope and assure me that my sins are forgiven; he gives me life anew and power in the Spirit, and a certain knowledge that, in the name and in the power of the blood of Christ, I can resist even the devil and he will flee from me. I am no longer in the hands and under the dominion of Satan; I am a child of God and a citizen of the kingdom of Christ.

That is the message! That is what he does to all who cry out unto him in their distress, and it is because he has done that to them that they praise him for his goodness and for his wonderful works to the children of men. It is because he has redeemed them and delivered them out of the hand of this terrible enemy.

Are you praising him for it? Have you been set free? You must agree that in my description I have been talking about you. This has not been a theoretical disquisition, has it? Have I not been describing your natural attitude towards God—the arrogance and the rebellion? Have I not been telling you how the devil has come and painted for you a marvellous picture of life and of liberty, and how you have believed him, and how you have become his slave, and how you find that it was not as wonderful as you thought it was? I have been speaking about you, slave of sin, slave of habits, slave of the devil.

But do you know the freedom? My dear friends, you have but one thing to do, and that is to acknowledge and confess the slavery, the folly, the ignorance, the arrogance. Confess it without reservation, and ask God if he will receive you and deliver you; and, as certainly as you do so, I promise you, he will tell you that he so loved you that he sent his only begotten Son into this world that you need not perish but have everlasting life.

You can come out of the prison-house now. The fetters can go, the bars of iron will be broken, the gates of brass will be shattered; Christ will lead you out and lead you the remainder of your life. And all he will expect from you is that you should praise him; that you should thank him, not only with your lips but with your life; that you will follow him, that you will tell everybody about him, and that you will be anxious that the poor slaves who are still in the prison-house may come out also.

It is inevitable, if you realise these things, that you must react like that. So I say to you now, cry out unto him, and if you do so I promise you he will in no wise cast you out. 'They cried unto the L<small>ORD</small> in their trouble' and (wonder of wonders!) 'he delivered them out of their distresses.' Oh, wondrous grace! Oh, ineffable love! Oh, everlasting mercy, that such a God should ever listen to the cry of such a sinner! But he has, and he will hear you. Cry out to him even now.

4
The dreadful disease

*'Fools because of their transgression,
and because of their iniquities, are afflicted. Their
soul abhorreth all manner of meat; and they draw near
unto the gates of death. Then they cry unto the* LORD *in
their trouble, and he saveth them out of their distresses. He sent
his word, and healed them, and delivered them from their
destructions. Oh that men would praise the* LORD *for
his goodness, and for his wonderful works to the children
of men! And let them sacrifice the sacrifices of thanksgiving,
and declare his works with rejoicing.'*
(Psalm 107:17-22)

Psalm 107 is a remarkable psalm judged from any standpoint. It is great as poetry. It is marvellous for its pictures, for the way in which it delineates situations. It is dramatic and descriptive purely as a piece of literature. It is well worthy of our careful consideration and analysis. But, of course, we are interested in it and concerned about it because of the truth that it contains, because of the message that it has for us. We have been looking at it in this way: the intention of the man who composed the psalm is that all people should praise God. God is to be praised because he is God, and the real essence of sin is not to praise God. That is where we all go so sadly astray when we tend to identify sin with particular sins. And that is why some people, of course, feel that they have never been sinners at all, because they have never done certain things.

If you would like to know whether you are a sinner or not, here is the test. Is the whole of your life given to the praise and the glory of God? If it is not, you are a sinner, and the Psalmist's case is that the whole of mankind is utterly helpless in its sin. It is the only cause of its trouble, though that one cause manifests itself in a large number of different ways. So the only hope for the world, says the writer, is in God, and it is only those who realise their utter hopelessness and helplessness, and who cry out unto the Lord in their trouble, who are delivered and set free. And then they will begin to praise God.

That is his thesis. Then, to prove his statement, he takes four examples and illustrations. He paints us four pictures which seem to be absolutely different from one another, and yet, if you take the trouble to read them carefully, you will find that there are certain phrases that come in every single picture. 'Then they cried unto the LORD in their trouble' (v.6); and 'he delivered them out of their distresses'(v.6); and 'Oh that men would praise the LORD for his goodness, and for his wonderful works to the children of men!' (v.8). In other words, his point is that though the pictures are apparently quite different, he then proves to you that they are identical.

We have already looked at the first two pictures, and now we come to the third. All these pictures, remember, are just representations of sin and of what sin does to us. The first is a picture of sin as it causes us to miss the mark and to go astray. The second is a picture of sin as slavery, which fetters us and dominates our lives. So where are we now? Well, we are no longer in a wilderness looking for a pathway, a great road going to a city, walking about so much that we are tired. Neither are we languishing or looking at men fettered to a wall with chains, languishing in corners in prison cells. No, we have gone upstairs, we are just in an ordinary bedroom, in an ordinary house, and we are looking at a poor person lying on a bed, obviously in a very serious condition.

The Psalmist is concerned to emphasise that on the surface the situation is absolutely different. It does not seem to have anything in common with the others. This is a very ordinary scene. So what is the picture this time? Well, obviously, it is a picture of sin as disease; sin as sickness; sin as the illness of the soul, the sickness of life, the sickness of mankind.

Picture 3—Disease

Now let us adopt the procedure we have adopted with the others. Let us, first of all, start with the picture and then go on to draw out the message and the lessons which it so clearly teaches. As in the previous instances, the terms are plain and very graphic. We are looking at sick patients, and let us observe them.

What does the Psalmist tell us about them? The first thing is that they are obviously ill and suffering from some sort of a disease. Not only that, he tells us that they are *afflicted*, which means that they look miserable and unhappy. Not only that, they are clearly suffering from pain. They are ill at ease and troubled.

Then we can go further. It is quite obvious to us from the Psalmist's description that they have lost their appetite: 'Their soul abhorreth all manner of meat' (v.18). They do not want any food, and if you bring food into the room, it makes them feel ill and violently sick; the sight of it upsets them. Not only do they not want it, they have a sense of revulsion against it. This is a very important part of the description. And, of course, as the result of all this, we read that 'they draw near to the gates of death.'

Wasting

The patients, in other words, are obviously suffering from some sort of a wasting disease. There are many causes of wasting diseases. It may be that they have some growth or some failure in the vital functions of the body. But whatever the precise cause is, the fact about these people is that they are desperately ill and sick. This condition of loss of appetite and revulsion against food, of course, has meant that they have become very thin and emaciated; and in addition to that, their colour is very pale, there seems to be no blood in their lips, and there is this awful pallor, this cachexia, the typical appearance of a person suffering from this kind of wasting disease. They also have no energy, so that they can scarcely move at all. Because of the lack of food and the loss of flesh, the nutriment which is normally required by the muscles and the nerves, and so on, is no longer there, and the heart in turn is suffering and is failing.

The result is this appalling picture of poor persons in a state of inertia, wasted and thin and pale and miserable, who gasp at every slightest move, and in whom the vital spark of life almost seems to have gone altogether. 'They draw near', as the Psalmist tells us, 'unto the [very] gates of death.' They have lost interest in everything; they are utterly miserable and unhappy. Everybody has been trying to do everything for them, but nothing can be done and they have given up all hope themselves.

Hopeless

It is a description of those who are in a completely hopeless state, wasting away in a kind of living death before your eyes, nothing but a kind of living skeleton. That is the picture which is drawn in these few graphic words and by these deft touches by the man who wrote this psalm. But you notice that he not only paints his picture, he also gives us the explanation of it. 'Fools because of their transgression, and because of their iniquities,' he says, are like that.

This is, perhaps, one of the commonest pictures of sin which is given in the Bible, both in the Old Testament and in the New. And it is, of course, a picture that suggests itself very readily to us: sin as sickness; sin as illness. There are those who recite Sunday by Sunday in their liturgy that 'there is no health in us'. That is their way of saying we are sinners. You will read in the Old Testament that it is said that Israel is sick 'from the sole of the foot to the head' (Isaiah 1:6) and that there is no health in him. And that is a marvellous representation of sin.

The Church, from the very beginning, has always adopted this picture; that is why people have always felt that in the New Testament leprosy is a very striking delineation of the effects of sin upon the soul of man. And there can be no doubt but that our blessed Lord and Saviour did many of his healing miracles with this double object and intent. It was to show his compassion, but above that it was to give a picture of sin and how he had come to deal with it. It was as if he said, 'I do this to the body, but I have come to do an infinitely bigger and greater thing for the soul. As this body suffered from physical disease and I have healed it, so the souls of men are suffering from a dreadful disease, a spiritual disease called sin, and I have come to heal them.' He used these very terms himself. He said, 'They that be whole need not a physician, but they that are sick' (Matthew 9:12).

Then, to look at it positively, what is the meaning of the term *salvation*? It means health. It means saving health. And the whole message of the New Testament, starting with Zacharias at the very beginning, is that the Lord Jesus Christ has come into the world in order to give us salvation: saving health, completeness, wholeness. Those are the terms and that is the meaning of holiness also.

The message

So having looked at the picture that is drawn by the Psalmist, let us now concentrate our attention upon the message, upon the doctrine.

Sin defined

What is he really telling us? Firstly, he tells us exactly what sin is. 'Fools because of their transgression, and because of their iniquities, are afflicted.' So here, the first thing we see about sin is that it is *transgression*. We saw earlier that it meant rebellion. It meant a contemptuous rejection of 'the counsel of the most High'. All these descriptions are true. There are many things to be said about sin, but now we are concentrating upon this one: transgression.

What does this mean? It means walking away from and ignoring and offending against what God meant for us. Transgression is deliberately going against that which God has indicated is his will and his way for us. Now, if we use this very illustration of health, I can show you this very simply. There are certain obvious laws of health and, if we want to enjoy health, then we must observe them. Certain things are absolutely essential to health—food, for instance. Food, solid and liquid, is necessary, and in exactly the same way fresh air is essential to health. Another essential is rest and sleep. If you go on working endlessly, then you are bound to suffer for it. So there are these certain laws that simply must be kept if we really are going to enjoy a state of health.

You can expand that for yourselves. As I say, if you do not eat enough your health will fail. On the other hand, if you eat too much you will also suffer. The law of health is that people should eat the right, the appropriate amount; never too little nor too much. And it is exactly the same with regard to rest and sleep. If you do not take any, then you may very well have a nervous breakdown. If you sleep too much you will be dull and lethargic, you will feel ill again and that will be the cause of your illness—too much sleep. And so on with all these other factors and various rules of health.

Now transgression means that we are not living according to those rules and laws; that we are violating them in some shape or form, or ignoring them; just as many people have done who eat too much, or drink too much, or who do not take sufficient rest. They work in the office all day, then dance or go to parties all night, or something like that. This goes on day after day and night after night, and at last they lose their health.

So if we are to understand sin, we must raise this into the spiritual realm, and it can be put very simply like this. God has made men and women for himself. He has made them to live according to certain laws and principles, and what the Bible tells us in utter simplicity is that if you and I do not live according to the laws and principles of our creation and of our nature, we shall suffer for it. It tells us that as people suffer in their physical health if they break the laws of physical health, so, if they do not conform to the laws and the arrangements that God has made for a total life as a spiritual being, it will lead to unhappiness, it will lead to misery, to affliction and to trouble. That is trangression. And it is because we transgress against the laws of our being that things go wrong with us. God has made us for himself. He so made us that we cannot thrive and flourish unless we are in the right correspondence with him and are receiving from him what he alone can give. If we do not do that we shall be afflicted.

Next, the term *iniquities* means crimes. Men and women in sin not only do not live as God meant them to live; they deliberately do things that are wrong. That is the difference between a transgression and a crime, between 'transgression' and 'iniquity'. Man in sin is not in a negative condition; it is not simply that he is not what God meant him to be; he is deliberately and actively something else. He has reduced himself to something else. He is guilty of crimes, a criminal. So that, according to the portion we are now considering, is what sin really is. That is what is afflicting us all.

Sinners described

But let us go to the second matter, which is this. What does the Bible say about the people who are afflicted because of transgressions and iniquities? And here the statement of the Psalmist is very important and specific. His first word is the word *fools*: 'Fools because of their transgression, and because of their iniquities . . .' However, we must understand exactly what the Psalmist does say. I am afraid this Authorised [King James] translation is not quite as

71

good as it might be at this point. A better translation is: 'Fools by their course [or by their way] of transgression and their iniquities, afflict themselves.' That is why they are fools. They bring their afflictions upon themselves. It is not that the afflictions come upon them because of what they have done, they produce their own affliction.

This is again, I suggest to you, the very first message of the Bible. Why is the world as it is? What has brought it to this? Why the tension? Why the trouble? Why the misunderstandings? Why the strain? Why is all that true both internationally and within the nation? Yes! let us be quite plain and specific: why is that true in the individual? Why is anybody unhappy? Why is anybody ill at ease? Why is anybody afflicted? Why are we all, by nature in this life and in this world, as we are and what we are? What is the matter with us? Is it some cursed fate? Is it some horrible spite of the unseen powers? And the answer of the Bible is quite simple and direct. We have brought it all upon ourselves. 'Fools because of their transgression, and because of their iniquities, afflict themselves.'

Let us be clear about this. The world is as it is because of the unutterable folly of man. It is not fate; it is not in our stars; it is not outside us; it is within us; it is we ourselves. Is that not the whole message of the Bible? The world was paradise, but it is no longer paradise. Why? Because man was a fool. He has brought it all upon himself, and this is something that we can never emphasise too much. So I want to emphasise this word *fools*. I know it is hated today. I know that it is utterly impossible for people to accept this biblical doctrine of sin. They say, 'I can't abide that teaching that we are sinners and that we are responsible for what we are. I do not believe . . .' But, whether you believe it or not, it is the simple truth about you. Every one of us is a fool, and this is how we show our folly. Sin really just means that we think that we know better than God.

That is what Adam did at the beginning. God gave him the ideal, perfect conditions, but he listened to a suggestion that there was a better way that God was withholding from him, and he went into it thinking that he was going to advance himself; thinking he was going to do something marvellous; and he did it! Oh, the fool! Because, in doing that, he has brought affliction upon himself, and it came almost at once. He did not know what to do with himself in his sin, and it is still the same. We are the architects of our own troubles. It is because we are what we are, and because we do and think the things that we do and think, that we are as miserable as we are and are surrounded by troubles and immersed in difficulties.

'Ah, but', you say, 'it is somebody else.' But the other person is saying exactly the same thing about you, and the fact of the matter is that it is true of all of us. It is because we are all self-centred and selfish; because we all think we are marvellous and that we know what to do. We can circumvent God's way. We have the mystic secret. We all believe it and we all practise it, and we bring our troubles headlong upon ourselves. 'Fools because of their transgression, and . . . iniquities, afflict themselves.'

In other words, there is nothing in the world that is so subtle as sin. Nobody, of course, ever sets out deliberately to afflict himself or herself. It is in our cleverness that we do it without realising what we are doing. We say we are 'out for a good time', and then we find ourselves in trouble. We did not go into trouble; we went in for a good time. But we have trouble because we have transgressed, we have ignored the laws. We have forgotten the principles of health. We say we were out for happiness, we really did not want to be miserable, we wanted to be happy.

And that is the extraordinary paradox of the world today. Look at your newspapers; see the accounts of the misery and the unhappiness. Stand on a street corner and just watch people. Why is the world so unhappy? In a sense, the answer is that they are all out for happiness. Everybody is chasing it and the result is unhappiness!

Why? Because we are not seeking it in the right way. That is the folly and the subtlety of sin. That is where we are deluded by it. We think we are out for the best; we find the worst.

Sin a robber

But let me work it out a little more in detail under a third principle, by asking you to consider with me the results to which sin inevitably always leads. I have already given you the answer in the picture: it is always this wasting disease; it is always this picture of that poor sick dying person lying so helplessly upon that bed.

To put it in the form of a principle, *sin always robs us and always takes away from us.* Do you not see there again the subtlety of it all? Sin comes to us as the best friend we have in the world who is offering us everything. And yet I assert this—and I shall prove it to you—that sin never gives us anything at all but invariably robs us. It is all in the parable of the Prodigal Son. There was a kind of life that appealed to him; it was going to give him so much. But from the moment that boy left home, he was being robbed, until at last he was penniless, sitting there in the field amidst the husks and the swine.

That is what sin always does. Forgive me if I use a kind of medical or, at any rate, pharmacological illustration. What I am trying to say is illustrated perfectly by alcohol. You ask a person what alcohol is and I think you will always find that they will say that alcohol is a stimulant. But pharmacologists do not classify alcohol as a stimulant; they always classify it—and rightly—as a depressant. 'Ah but', you say, 'that is impossible; alcohol does stimulate us. If a man is tired and he drinks a glass of whisky he feels full of energy, he is brightened and he is enlivened. Surely, alcohol must be a stimulus!' But it is not. What that alcohol does to you is this: it knocks out your highest faculties, your highest centres. It knocks out all control, in other words, and the result is that a kind of elemental power which is within you, that is normally balanced,

74

becomes imbalanced and you feel you have more energy. But you do not have any more energy at all. Alcohol, by knocking off the control, has released something for the time being, and at the end you are more exhausted than you were before. How subtle it is!

Let me put it to you again in terms of pharmacology. Any alcoholic drink always makes one feel much warmer; that is common knowledge, is it not? Yes, but if you read the textbooks, indeed if you listen to the advice of people, you will find that they always tell you never to take alcohol before you are going out into the cold air. Why not? Because what alcohol does to you is not, as you think, to increase the heat that is in you; what it is really doing is to dilate your surface vessels, and you have a sensation of heat because you are losing heat. So the alcohol does not give you more heat; it drains you of heat and gives you a pleasant, warm and comfortable feeling because you are emanating heat for the time being; and in the end you are much colder and, therefore, more subject to a chill.

Now that is a perfect picture of sin. Sin always robs and takes from us. Let me suggest some of the things which it takes that are suggested to me by this picture.

Sin always robs us of innocence. Adam and Eve were innocent until they sinned. The moment they listened to the devil they lost their innocence. Do not misunderstand me: I do not accept the philosophy of the late J. M. Barrie with his *Peter Pan,* but there is such a thing, after all, as a relative innocence at any rate, and we all start in this world with that. But the moment you sin you have lost it. It robs us of innocence; it robs us of purity; it robs us of refinement. The moment we play with sin and commit it, we have lost a certain refinement. A certain coarseness always comes in when you sin. You see it in people's faces, do you not? What a terrible thing sin is! How it coarsens the very complexion, thickens the visage, as it were! A man cannot go on sinning but that it will show itself in his eyes, in his skin, in his hands; everywhere in his body there is a coarseness, a roughness. It robs us of refinement and delicacy.

Not only that, *sin always robs us of balance and of judgement.* That is, I suggest, the sole explanation of the supposed brilliance of the after-dinner speaker who has taken a little drink. It is not that he has been unusually brilliant, it is that he has been saying things which normally he would not have said because the alochol has knocked out his control, and the same has happened to the people who are listening to him. So they are all in that state in which they do not have a perfect balance and judgement, and they think it is marvellous. They say they cannot be convivial without drink, and that means that while they are normal and controlled they cannot be convivial. They have to be drugged before they can be released. So it robs us of balance and judgement; and that is why some of us would be prepared to support an Act of Parliament which says that anyone who has taken even the slightest amount of alcohol should never be allowed to be in charge of a motor car. The moment you take even the smallest amount in, it has affected your judgement. You do not see things straightly, you have lost your balance.

Not only that, *sin robs us of inward peace.* The moment you sin, conscience begins to work and you are unhappy. How unhappy Adam and Eve were the moment they had sinned! And it is the same with all of us. It was marvellous before, and there was nothing but joy and happiness and a great thrill; but the moment you do it, there is a reaction and a revulsion and you are unhappy and are filled with remorse. I need not stay with these things; it is enough to mention them. You have lost your peace. You lose your joy. And indeed, if you continue in it you will even lose your physical health.

But still more tragic and devastating about sin is that *it robs us of our taste for good things.* People who live a life of sin see nothing in the Bible and in good books. They do not appreciate the life of

a saint. The saint is a bore to them. They have lost their appreciation of all that is good and noble and uplifting. They even lose their
taste for poetry and for music and all these things. They must have
this stimulus all along.

But this picture suggests something even more remarkable than
that about sin. Habitual and confirmed sinners not only lose their
taste for good things, *they even lose their taste for bad things.* Had
you ever thought of that? They get tired of them, and that is why
they have to change their sins. I remember a poor man once who
was a drug-taker, and do you know why that man had taken to
drugs? This was his story, and it was the simple truth. He had drunk
so much that he (to use his own language) could 'no longer get a
kick out of it'. He had finished that, as it were, so he had to take to
drugs. He got no pleasure any longer out of drink, so he had to go
to something else, and you will find that they always do that. It is
the state of lifelessness. They have been so stimulating themselves
falsely, in the way I have described to you, that they have been
robbed of their vital energy, and they need something more and
more powerful as they go on.

There is a poem which gives a much better picture than I can
ever paint to you of the way in which sin so robs us that in the end
it leaves us just an empty husk of life with nothing at all. I shall
quote two verses from the poet Byron, a man who had his fill of sin
and of what this world can give. A great poet, I admit, a genius, yes,
but not a Christian; a sinner, a man of the world, a transgressor.
Now in 1824 he celebrated his thirty-sixth birthday and he wrote a
poem entitled, 'On this day I complete my thirty-sixth year.' That
is a comparatively young age, but here is a man who has been living a godless, worldly life for most of those thirty-six years, and
this is what he says:

> *My days are in the yellow leaf;*

He is only thirty-six, remember!

The flowers and fruits of love are gone;

He had had his fill of love. He was the great lover, the Don Juan, was he not? A marvellous lover, but at the age of thirty-six he says,

> *The flowers and fruits of love are gone;*
> *The worm, the canker and the grief*
> *Are mine alone!*

What an appalling condition to be in at such a young age! But, of how many has that been true!

> *The fire that on my bosom preys*
> *Is lone as some volcanic isle;*
> *No torch is kindled at its blaze,*
> *A funeral pile.*

Poor Byron! Exhausted to such a degree and to such a point at the age of thirty-six! His days are already as the yellow leaf. The flowers and the fruits have gone; the excitement and the thrill and the abandon and the joy have long since been forgotten. 'Their soul abhorreth all manner of meat; and they draw near unto the gates of death.' He is not only sick of sin, he is sick of life. It is ended; it is a funeral pile; the husk is left, the kernel has gone. He is burnt out; he is exhausted; there is nothing left. Sin has robbed him of everything and he can find no kick in life. Nothing can stimulate him. Love, even the thing he lived for, has gone. He is on the scrap heap of life.

'Fools because of their transgression, and because of their iniquities, afflict themselves. Their soul abhorreth all manner of meat; and they draw near unto the gates of death.' Exhausted. Lifeless. Hopeless. Tired of life. Dying with nothing whatsoever. Robbed and penniless.

That is what sin does. It reduces us to refuse and throws us onto the scrap heap. Do you not see that in all this, as I expound this psalm, I am simply putting in my language and in biblical language what you can read in the newspapers whenever you like? It is all there! You live that kind of life and that will be the result. So thank God that we have a gospel! 'Their soul abhorreth all manner of meat; and they draw near unto the gates of death. Then they cry unto the LORD in their trouble, and he saveth them out of their distresses' (vv.18-19).

Healing and deliverance

Is it possible? Is it possible that this person who is dying there, being eaten by the canker, losing all vitality and health and strength and power—is it possible that anything can be done? It is! 'He sent his word, and healed them, and delivered them from their destructions' (v.20). 'Oh that men would praise the LORD for his goodness, and for his wonderful works to the children of men!' (v.8).

What does it mean? It is the old, old story of the gospel. They cried out, and what did God do? 'He sent his word, and healed them.' What is the word? The word of the gospel. The apostle Peter talks about it in his first Epistle; 'This is the word which by the gospel is preached unto you' (1 Peter 1:25). The reconciling word. It is what Christ does. He did it to the nobleman's son. He simply sent a word and it happened (John 4:46-50). It is the same thing! He is the Word of God and he has come into the world in order to heal this fell disease.

And how has he done it? He first of all deals with the infection, or the growth, the canker, or whatever it may be, and he takes it out of us. He extirpates it and stops the disease process.

Guilt removed

The first need of men and women is that the guilt of sin be removed, that the poison be taken out. And he came from heaven

79

to earth in order to do it. If I may use such a phrase, he came to suck the poison of this terrible disease out of us, and it meant his own death, but he died that you and I might be forgiven. He died that we might be reconciled to God. And his word is 'the word of reconcil-iation', that 'God was in Christ, reconciling the world unto himself, not imputing their trespasses unto them' (2 Corinthians 5:19).

Health restored

But, thank God, he did not stop at that! Healing means much more than that. It means the restoration of health. 'He sent his word, and healed them', and Christ does it in this way. This New Testament doctrine does not merely tell us that our sins are forgiven; it goes on to tell us that we are given new life. Its doctrine is what it calls the doctrine of rebirth and of regeneration. We can be born again. He injects, as it were, new life into us. He gives us a new start. He rescues us from the very jaws of death and the grave and hell, and then he gives us life anew. We become new men and women. He puts us upon our feet. We have new vigour, new powers, new tastes, new desires. He fills us with a new kind of life and of exis-tence altogether. That is how he heals.

> *He breaks the power of cancelled sin,*
> *He sets the prisoner free.*
>   Charles Wesley

He gives us that divine life and makes us 'partakers of the divine nature' (2 Peter 1:4). We are new creations: 'old things are passed away; behold, all things are become new' (2 Corinthians 5:17).

We are taken off the bed, out of the bedroom, put in the open air, given the tasks and given the power to perform them. And not only that, he fills us with an abundant and an abounding health and joy. Did you notice how the Psalmist puts it? 'He sent his word, and healed them, and delivered them from their destructions. Oh that men would praise the Lord for his goodness, and for his wonderful works to the children of men! And let them sacrifice the sacrifices of thanksgiving, and declare his works with rejoicing' (vv.20-22).

The Lord Jesus Christ does not merely tide you over the crisis and make you feel a little bit better on that sick bed. Not at all! He has dealt with the disease. He gives you new life, and it is so marvellous and so thrilling that whereas you were hopeless and exhausted and, like Byron, with your life at its 'yellow leaf', you are now the exact opposite. 'I am come', says the Lord Jesus Christ, 'that they might have life'. But he did not stop there: 'I am come that they might have life, and that they might have it more abundantly' (John 10:10). A superabundance of life and of health, of vigour and of power, joy and rejoicing, where formerly there was misery and wretchedness. 'Beauty for ashes . . . the garment of praise for the spirit of heaviness' (Isaiah 61:3). The spirit of rejoicing in place of heaviness. A real health, a vigorous personality. Not a mere weakling shuffling through life, but one who is filled with the power of the Spirit, and rejoicing as he goes on living in Christ Jesus. That is the message!

My friend, my friend, how are you? What do you feel like? Are you on your feet in life, or are you lying on that sick bed? Are you tired, are you weary spiritually? Are you exhausted? Have you lost interest in life? Have you sometimes said to yourself, 'Wish I were dead!'? How many say that today!—'Wish I were dead. Wish I could get out of it.' Have you lost vitality? Have you lost pleasure? Have you lost everything? Are you merely existing, slowly dying, your vitality being eaten out as by a cancer within you?

If you are, and if you are tired of trying to rouse yourself and to heal yourself, and if you have given up turning to the world and its methods, it is my privilege to tell you this in utter simplicity: Cry out unto the Lord! He is the only one who can deal with you. I do not care what your circumstances are. You can tell me about your problems and your difficulties, but I don't care what they are.

When he replies, he delivers. He will heal you. He will reconcile you unto himself. He will let you know that he has done it. You will know that your sins are forgiven, and you will be amazed at yourself. You will have a new life; you will be a new person; you will have new interests, new joys, and you will not understand yourself. It is because he will have given you this gift of life, of health, of wholeness, of mastery. And he will sustain you and feed you and help you to live according to his laws and principles of spiritual health while you remain in this world, and afterwards receive you unto himself and usher you into the endless glory.

It grieves me to think that there is even the possibility of anybody going out of this service still feeling unhappy, feeling miserable, feeling lifeless, and feeling defeated. My dear friend, like all these people, cry out unto the Lord in your trouble, and he will deliver you out of your distresses. Acknowledge and confess that you are as you are because of your own sin; repent, acknowledge it, confess it. Do not plead anything, but admit it all, and then believe him when he tells you that he sent his Son to die for you and for your sins, and that he will give you life anew.

Repent. Believe. And you will prove it to be true.

5
The terrible storm

'They that go down to the sea in ships, that do
business in great waters; these see the works of the LORD,
and his wonders in the deep. For he commandeth, and raiseth the
stormy wind, which lifteth up the waves thereof. They mount up to
the heaven, they go down again to the depths: their soul is melted
because of trouble. They reel to and fro, and stagger like a drunken
man, and are at their wit's end. Then they cry unto the LORD in
their trouble, and he bringeth them out of their distresses. He
maketh the storm a calm, so that the waves thereof are still.
Then are they glad because they be quiet; so he bringeth them
unto their desired haven. Oh that men would praise the LORD
for his goodness, and for his wonderful works to the children
of men! Let them exalt him also in the congregation of
the people, and praise him in the assembly of the elders.'
(Psalm 107:23-32)

The Psalmist is showing us, you remember, that sin does not always manifest itself in the same way. It takes different forms. You go around a hospital ward, and you look at the man in bed number one. There he is, propped up and gasping for breath; he has penumonia and is desperately ill. Look at the man in bed number two: he is lying flat on his back; there is no movement whatsoever, no struggle. Indeed, the difficulty is to decide whether he is still alive or not. Is he still breathing? He seems to be so quiet. Yes, but the point is, you see, that they are both ill. They are both in a diseased condition. It is not the difference between the

83

dramatic manifestations of disease and the quietness of another that matters; the common thing is that both are diseased and both are equally helpless, unless something drastic is done and the right medicament is applied. That is precisely this man's case in this hundred and seventh psalm.

Picture 4—The Storm

So we come to the fourth, his last picture, and now we are no longer in a wilderness or a prison cell or a sick bedroom. Where are we? We are on the high seas, in mid-ocean; and he proceeds to give us his dramatic and his most graphic and living picture of the whole situation. It is a picture of a terrible storm at sea. We see a boat on the ocean, and it is in terrible trouble, buffeted, beaten and battered by these raging billows and by the howling gale. Notice how the Psalmist puts it: 'He commandeth, and raiseth the stormy wind, which lifteth up the waves thereof' (v.25). Have you seen the Atlantic rollers? Have you seen those gigantic waves coming, rising like mountains and hurling themselves? That is what he is talking about. And they are hurling themselves at that little ship.

Then he proceeds to a description of the people on board the ship, and it is rather important that we should realise that the next thing he says really refers to the people and not to the waves. Verse 26 reads, 'They mount up to the heaven, they go down again to the depths.' Now that is not a description of the waves, although it is true of them also. No, he is describing the man in the boat, because he goes on, 'They mount up to heaven, they go down again to the depths: their soul is melted because of trouble.' And anybody who has been in a storm at sea knows exactly what this means. You are raised up by that terrific wave, and then down you go again; you are up and you are down, backwards and forwards. It is a perfect description of what takes place under such terrifying conditions.

So there they are, and he tells us not only that 'their soul is melted because of trouble'; they are in a state of acute distress.

They are apparently at the mercy of these breakers and they do not know what to do. They are up and they are down. And not only that. He then comes to a more minute and accurate description of these people. He says that 'They reel to and fro, and stagger like a drunken man.' They are not drunk, they are perfectly sober; but because of what is happening to them and to the boat, they cannot balance themselves and they are hurled against corridors from side to side, and from partition to partition. You look at them and you say, 'That man is drunk, he has lost his balance.' But no, it is the storm. It is the action of these billows, buffeting and battering away at the ship.

Then, finally, he tells us that they are 'at their wit's end'. It is very important we should understand that. He means that they do not know what to do; that every possibility they can think of has been absolutely exhausted. It is a picture of complete hopelessness. Everything that can be done by mariners and navigators and all who are experts in these matters has been done, but it avails them nothing. It is no use giving instructions. They have been given and they have been carried out, but nothing happens. The ship is helpless, at the mercy of the waves, and it is on the point of going down at any moment; they do not know what will happen. And, of course, they are far away from that haven for which they originally set out. They are abandoned to their fate, and the next thing you expect to hear is that suddenly the ship is engulfed by some particularly gigantic wave, or that she has split in two; and down she goes out of sight, and is swallowed up and never seen again.

But, of course, that is not what he tells us; he tells us that at the height of this storm, and in the utter calamity in which they are placed, 'They cry unto the LORD in their trouble, and he bringeth them out of their distresses. He maketh the storm a calm, so that the waves thereof are still. Then are they glad because they be quiet; so he bringeth them unto their desired haven.'

Now, again, this is nothing but a very dramatic Old Testament representation of the message of the gospel of our Lord and Saviour Jesus Christ. The Psalmist was, first and foremost, dealing with facts, but his whole purpose in writing the psalm is perfectly obvious, if you read the whole of it: it is to give the message of salvation. His point is that whatever your predicament, whatever your position, if you do genuinely cry out unto the Lord, he will deliver you.

There is another illustration of this in the New Testament. It is in Mark's Gospel and it tells how our Lord was in a boat with the disciples on one occasion. He was tired and he was asleep in the stern of the vessel. Then the storm arose and the waves were rising and the water was coming in, so the disciples tried baling it out. But things were going from bad to worse, and they rushed to him and said, 'Master, carest thou not that we perish? And he arose, and rebuked the wind, and said unto the sea, Peace, be still. And . . . there was a great calm' (Mark 4:38,39). This was perfectly true, an event in history, something that actually happened. Yes, but it is also a picture, and it is the truth that is pictured in this way that really matters. That is the whole of salvation, it is the message of the Christian gospel to this world today.

The gospel message

So what does it mean? First, let me put it in a slightly different way and present it to you as the gospel message. This is just another of the four pictures which the Psalmist gives us of life as a result of sin. If you would like it in a more particular manner, we can put it like this: it is a picture of frail men and women facing and battling with the storms of life. That is what he has here, so that he is no longer painting a picture of sin as missing the mark, nor of sin as slavery and bondage, nor of sin as a disease that robs us and eats out the vitals of our spiritual nature. I think that here he is depicting to us the violent character of sin; the turmoil to which sin inevitably and always leads.

Turmoil

Now this is a very common picture in the Bible and it is also, because of that, a very common picture in our hymns. The hymn-writers have been very quick to take it up because it lends itself so perfectly to the presentation of the gospel. It is a picture of life in this world as a kind of voyage. What is your birth? Well, it is nothing but embarking; you step on board ship and the ship goes out of the harbour and faces the ocean. And the picture, generally, goes on like this. At first the sea is delightfully calm; the sun is shining, the band is playing, and we look forward to a marvellous voyage. It is the first time we have ever taken it. We have never been on board before, there are many other passengers with us and we are looking forward to this marvellous time with the keenest anticipation. There we are in our youth, and off we go quite confident that nothing can ever go wrong; nothing will ever happen; there will never be another cloud; nothing can hide that gorgeous, bright sunshine, because it is so powerful.

And the sea? Why, it is as smooth as silk! Nothing can ever cause a ripple on the surface of such a smooth sea. We shall be fortunate; we have heard of people in the past who have got into trouble, and we have heard of storms and the need of lifeboats and things like that. Ah well, of course, they were a little bit unfortunate, but in our case it will obviously be so different. Nothing can go wrong; nothing will go wrong. It will be marvellous, and we settle down. There are new discoveries. There are new mechanisms on the boat. There are things which our forefathers knew nothing at all about, and with these things, well, it does not matter very much what happens.

You remember how, in the case of the Titanic, for instance, we were given the assurance that nothing could sink that ship. 'But what about icebergs?' said somebody. 'Well,' they said, 'of course, we know all about icebergs, but this is a ship inside a ship, so that if it should crash into an iceberg, the outer shell will go but the inner shell will still remain.' The unsinkable ship! The latest advances of science! We are always advancing and, therefore, we have every reason for believing that nothing will go wrong in this voyage on which we have embarked.

Am I just romancing? Am I just drawing on my imagination? Consult your own life. Go back to your own experience. We all start with this idea that for some reason or another things are going to be different with us. And off we go!

But that is not the end of the story, unfortunately. Let me come to the teaching, the message, and it is this: we have not gone very far before we begin to find that that sea does not remain calm and smooth. There are ripples. There are disturbances. You get up in the morning and you read the report which says 'Slight swell'. Then you go on a bit further and it says, 'Somewhat choppy', and so on. And on you go from stage to stage, and you begin to make the discovery that it looks as if your experience will be very similar, after all, to that which has happened to those who have gone before you.

Not smooth sailing
Let me put it to you in a more doctrinal form. Life is not smooth sailing. The Bible starts by telling us that, and that is why this is the Word of God. Do you see? Everything has always tried to persuade us that all will be smooth sailing. In spite of everything that is true of the world at this moment, it still has the idea that somehow it can all be put right, and that there really is the possibility of an existence in this world in which there will never be any more trouble. The world believes that. It is its fatal optimism, based upon its ignorance of sin.

But the Bible does not say that. The Bible meets us with a stark honesty at the very beginning and says that life is a place of trouble. Life is a stormy sea. Oh, you may not like that, or you may say that it is depressing. But it is not a question of hurling epithets about; the question is, What are the facts? Read the history books and bring their report to the light of the Bible and of other literature. Here is the truth. Life is a stormy sea and we go on in this condition. Why? Well, the cause of the trouble, says the Bible, is still the same. It is what it calls sin. It was not meant to be like this, but it is like this because of man's original disobedience.

How simple, how direct is the Scripture! People are saying that this or that is the trouble. No, no! says the Bible, the trouble is man's disobedience against God and nothing else. That is what started the disturbance; that is what set this course going. And God's reply to that, as it were, in his justice and in his holiness, is, 'He commandeth, and raiseth the stormy wind, which lifteth up the waves thereof' (v.25). It is a profound mystery, but it is true. The world was never meant to be like this; life was never meant to be like this; but it is so because of man's sin and his disobedience.

But someone may say to me, 'What do you mean by these storms of life?' Let me put it in a more experimental manner. Shall I remind you of some of the things that have put you into this condition of reeling and staggering like a drunken man? Shall I tell you what has constituted the billows and these tremendous waves in your life that have rocked you right and left and backwards and forwards? What are the things that shake us, the storms of life?

Storms within and without
Think of those *within* you to start with. Think of the storm of passion. It shakes you. Have you not seen people shaking and trembling in the storm and wave of passion? Anger, temper. And then the waves, the billows of that other type of passion—lust. Lust almost driving you, carrying you along; this wave, this billow has flung you over, and you are like a little ship, helpless.

There is a hymn that talks about 'the storms of passion and self-will'. Have you seen a child standing up in rebellion against its parent, wanting to do something but the parent says no? It is a storm. It is just nothing but the rising of these great billows hurling backwards and forwards. The child is in the grip of this; the parent perhaps at the same time. Have you not known these things inside you that rise as veritable waves? They seem to rise from nowhere and yet they are there; and we scarcely know where we are or what we are doing.

But think of those that come *from the outside*. Think of temptations. You are going along apparently quite calmly; you may be in an excellent frame of mind. You may have been reading your Bible; you may have been praying to God. You may have been spending your time with some loved one; you may have been talking about them as beautiful things in life. You may have been looking at a great picture or listening to some marvellous music, and you are calm and quiet and you are walking home. And—suddenly!—you are hit and struck by a wave of temptation before you know where you are. This is life, isn't it?

You did not think there was going to be a storm that night, did you? No, no! The disciples did not think there would be a storm when they took the boat that day on the Lake of Galilee. The characteristic of that lake was that, suddenly, from nowhere, a wind would come and the storm would have been upon you. And so it comes in temptation and suggestion and innuendo in this city of London and elsewhere. These waves of temptation that reach you so unexpectedly in life!

But think of it in terms of trials and troubles. Think of it in the form of illness. Think of it in terms of some financial loss or the loss of your work, or something like that. You are going on, maintaining the even tenor of your way; or, to use the nautical comparison again, maintaining an even keel, and you thought that all was well. Suddenly, down you have gone: you are taken ill, you are lying on your bed, and you are wondering what is going to happen next. Or you have lost your post, or you have lost your money, or somebody has let you down, or there has been some treachery. The list of these different things that come in these various ways and attack us is almost endless.

And then rumours of wars. Actual wars, twice already in this twentieth century. Look at life as it was in the early months even of 1914. Who would have thought a storm was coming? The sea had never been smoother. The prosperity of Great Britain had never been so great. The whole world was advancing, it was in a marvellous condition. We were settling down to enjoy ourselves on the sun-deck of life. And suddenly it came from apparently nothing: something that happened in a little country like Serbia; and the World War came and the billows were rising upon us and we were shaking and rocking in a great convulsion in mid-ocean. And it was exactly the same in 1939.

And what of it today? We are on a stormy sea; we are hearing about atomic powers and possibilities. We need not stay with this. People today are prepared to listen to great philosophers. I understand that Bertrand Russell wrote a letter to the *Manchester Guardian* [now the *Guardian*] in which he said that unless this crisis over Formosa [now Taiwan] is settled we will probably all be dead before the end of this year. That is not my opinion; it is his. And if that is not a storm, what is? You see them rise, the waves and the billows, and they hurl themselves; and here is a little barque. You have set out in life—I am speaking to younger people particularly at this moment—did you ever think you were going to be in a world like that, or a life like that? These things are outside you and your whole future is uncertain and you wonder what is going to happen.

At the mercy of life
But the thing I want to emphasise is this: that what all this leads to is the sense of our being at the mercy of life, and at the mercy of the great powers that are operating in this life and in this world. The picture which this man gives is one of a little boat that is

absolutely helpless. It is at the mercy of the waves and the billows and the raging of the wind and of the storm. Now the Bible tells us that that is what sin always leads to, and that we do not master life; life masters us. We are not in control, but we are being controlled by other forces and factors within us and outside us. We are being buffeted and we are being battered. We are being thrown hither and thither.

I know that everybody does not agree with this. Henley the poet wrote:

> *Out of the night that covers me,*
> *Black as the Pit from pole to pole,*
> *I thank whatever gods may be*
> *For my unconquerable soul.*

He says, 'Whatever you may say, my soul is unconquerable—it will never be mastered.'

> *In the fell clutch of circumstance,*
> *I have not winced nor cried aloud:*
> *Under the bludgeonings of chance*
> *My head is bloody, but unbowed.*

But, alas, poor Henley made an admission without realising it. What I would like to have asked Henley was this. If he was so much and so entirely in control, how comes it that his head is bloody? Why is the blood pouring down his forehead and down his face? 'Under the bludgeonings of chance'—that is what I am saying: he has been bludgeoned; he has been battered and buffeted; he has been bruised. 'My head is bloody'—I am wounded. The man who set out in the sunshine, and who was so certain that nothing would ever go wrong, who was in charge and in control! But listen to him as he goes on:

> *It matters not how strait the gate,*
> *How charged with punishments the scroll,*
> *I am the master of my fate:*
> *I am the captain of my soul.*
>
> William Ernest Henley, 1849–1903

Poor fool! Master of his fate? Well then, I ask again, why is his head bleeding? Why can he not stop the raging of the sea? Why can he not produce a calm? Why can he not arrive at his haven? Is he the captain of his soul? Is he the pilot? Is his engine still working? Is his compass still in line? What about his logbook? Where is he? He does not know.

No, no! All that was so written by Henley is nothing but the picture of a man whistling in the dark, trying to keep up his courage. He has no idea where he is going. He has no control whatsoever over his life and over his fate. And to talk about being the captain of his soul! He is not in control at all. It is the other things—lust and passion and desire, temptation—these things; and then trials and troubles and tribulations. That is it!

At wit's end

The Psalmist's picture is absolutely perfect. What do these things all lead to? Well, 'They reel to and fro, and stagger like a drunken man.' What a wonderful description that is! As men and women go on in life and experience these things, they begin to be conscious of a loss of grip and a loss of control. They talked a lot at one time about their will-power and that they could do anything they wanted to do, but they find that will-power is not as powerful as they thought it was. They are losing grip. They are losing control. At first, it is very light and superficial, but it gets worse. They begin to stagger. Then everything becomes uncertain and they are reeling about; they do not know where they are. They have lost their sense of direction. They have completely lost control.

But what I want to emphasise above everything else is that we are told that they are 'at their wit's end', and that is the most important message of all. It is just the Bible's way of saying that face to face with life as it is, human wisdom is completely useless. That is all it means. At their wit's end. What is wit? It is a man's wisdom, his knowledge, his understanding. It is his ability, his power to plan, his power to apply remedies. That is his wit. A man lives by his wits; his knowledge, his keenness, his intellect, his understanding.

So if these people are at their wit's end, it means they have done everything they can and it does not avail them. They have thought it out. They say, 'What can we do? Throw a little of the luggage overboard. Lighten the ship. Pull down a sail; put up another. Change the rigging.' All these various things. 'Change the course.' They have done it all. They are at their wit's end.

Now that is a fundamental proposition of the whole Bible. It is just to say that men and women in life in this world, as the result of sin, are completely and entirely baffled. Oh, they have been doing many things through many centuries to try to steady this ship of life. Read the philosophers and poets. Read about the scientific advancements. Read the biographies of statesmen. Go to your international conferences. What are they about? They are simply trying to control the ship in the storm, and somehow to produce order and calm. They are doing it still.

But the Bible's diagnosis and pronouncement is that they do not understand. They are at their wit's end; they do not know the cause of the trouble and, therefore, they obviously cannot apply the remedy. So all their schemes lead to nothing. In spite of their optimistic prophecies, nothing eventuates. Man has done his all, his utmost; he is exhausted. All his thinking and his brilliance, and still the storm is raging more hotly than ever. Is not that the position?

And so the soul of mankind becomes melted in trouble. The average person today has a sense of utter and complete futility about life. They are absolutely hopeless; they say that we are drifting to disaster; the end must be coming; nothing can be done. There is nothing left but to be drowned. The utter collapse of civilisation. Everything is going down into this final disaster. We are sinking. Is that not it?

And the Bible says it is, and the history of the world proves that it is. Is there no hope therefore? I have already given you the answer. It is here in every one of the pictures. 'They cried unto the LORD in their trouble, and he saved them out of their distresses.' They were on the point of sinking. No sign of the harbour. No sign of the haven. Lost in mid-Atlantic as it were, and on the point of going down. Civilisation is like that. The world is like that. The individual man or woman is like that. They do not know where they are. They have lost their bearings. They cannot see the Northern Star. The moon seems to have gone, to be entirely eclipsed. The sun has not been seen for days. There is a mist. Everything has gone wrong. Where are we? We do not know! And we are on the point of going down. But then there are certain people who cry out unto the Lord, and 'he delivers them out of their distresses'.

Deliverance

That is the whole story of Christianity; the story of the coming of the Son of God into the world. When all was lost,

> *When all was sin and shame,*
> *A second Adam to the fight*
> *And to the rescue came.*
> John Henry Newman

Take this picture. There is that little ship, helpless, on the point of going down. The Master and everybody else have given up hope. The Captain has given up. Abandon ship! Hopeless! Then, suddenly and unexpectedly, and in an apparently miraculous manner, the pilot steps on board, and immediately everything is changed. Listen to this dramatic description: 'He maketh the storm a *calm,* so that the waves thereof are still. Then are they glad because they be quiet; so he bringeth them unto their desired haven' (vv.29,30).

'Ah,' says someone, 'a fairy tale, poetic imagination! It isn't true!' But it is the simple truth. This is Christian experience. This is the very thing he does. The most amazing thing of all is that he ever comes. Why did God not abandon the world to itself? It had sinned against him. It had produced its own misery, and there it is, reaping the consequences of its own action. Why does he bother? Why has he ever looked upon it? But he does. That is the message: 'For God so loved the world . . .' (John 3:16).

Calm

He sees the ship there in mid-ocean; he sees what is happening, and he sends his only Son. He has done it! And what I read is this: 'He maketh the storm a calm'. And that is what the Lord Jesus Christ always does. The moment you meet him, the first thing that happens to you is that you are conscious of a calm. He put it in the form of an invitation, didn't he? He said, 'Come unto me, all ye that labour and are heavy laden, and I will give you rest' (Matthew 11:28). Calm. Peace.

How does he do it? Well, time fails me, but this is the essence of the gospel message. The moment, in your distresses and in your agony, you turn to him, you are at once conscious that the whole situation is somehow different. Why? Well, there is something about him. He seems to know. He seems to understand. He seems to have a knowledge. He seems to have a power. He seems to have an ability. Have you not had some experience of that kind of thing when you have been struggling over something? I could give you endless illustrations. Do you remember when, as a child, you were trying to work out your problems in arithmetic or geometry, or something else? You could not do it at all and you were becoming desperate and frantic, and somebody came along who understood. 'It's all right,' he said, 'now let me see. This is the first line . . .' And then it seemed so simple and the whole thing was solved. Calm!

Or have you not had it sometimes when perhaps you were faced with some problem and you did not know what to do, and you, too, were at your wit's end? A friend suddenly appeared and said, 'It's all right; now wait a moment . . .' And your agitation has already gone.

Or it may be like this. I remember once watching a man trying to do an operation. The poor man was not very expert and he was in great trouble and confusion. Another surgeon happened to come in and he said, 'Now what is happening here?' Then he mopped up here, and he opened that, and the whole thing became plain, and how simple it seemed! He was a master, and when a master operates, you feel you could do it equally well.

It is the same in every area of life; that is the sort of calmness that a master produces. So when, in the midst of life, you feel you are about to sink, and you meet Christ, you feel at once that here is somebody who knows. Here is somebody who understands. Here is someone who has faced the storm at its most desperate, with all the billows of hell howling at him, but he went through them all and came to the haven successfully. And he has stepped on board. He is in control. He understands. He masters life. He knows what he is doing.

I say I am troubled about my past. I cannot get rid of that billow that seems to be coming from behind me and shaking my little barque. 'It is all right', he says, 'I have died for you. I gave my life for that sin. I have made myself responsible for you. Your past is blotted out, it is forgiven.' And then I say, 'Look at this one coming on the side. How can I live in the present?' He says, 'I am going to be with you.' 'Look at those coming in the future. I see them coming at me. I must go down.' 'No, no,' he says, 'I will never leave thee, nor forsake thee' (Hebrews 13:5).

Is that not what he does? It does not matter what direction the storm comes from. It matters not where the billows rise. When he is on board there is a calm.

> *Safe in the arms of Jesus,*
> *Safe on his gentle breast.*
> Frances Jane Van Alstyne

Or, as the Old Testament puts it, in the midst of the storm and everything, when the foundation seems to have gone, 'Underneath are the everlasting arms' (Deuteronomy 33:27), and they will never fail.

Or the other word which the Psalmist uses is the word *quiet*: 'Then are they glad because they be quiet.' And that means Christ's all-sufficiency for every occasion and every eventuality. I like the way Paul puts this point. 'For I have learned,' he says, 'in whatsoever state I am, therewith to be content' (Philippians 4:11). Quiet. A quiet mind. A quiet heart. Like the man in Psalm 112:7 who is 'not afraid of evil tidings'. Why? Because he has a quiet and a peace within that nothing can disturb. He has a new view of life; a new insight into the whole course of history. He knows that he is right with God and, therefore, whatever happens in this world, he is right eternally. Quiet! 'Then are they glad because they be quiet.' 'I can do all things through Christ, which strengtheneth me' (Philippians 4:13).

Journey's end
Then, at the end, 'He bringeth them unto their desired haven' (v.30). He gives me a new life, yes, and a new sense of direction. He helps me to understand this Book, which is God's logbook in the voyage of life. I see my way; I can chart my course; I know where not to go and what to avoid; I go straight on and he is with me. He will never leave me. He is the pilot of my barque. I am in

him and he is in me, and he fills me with his Spirit, and he will keep his hand upon me and upon the vessel until he has piloted me into the eternal harbour.

I generally close the morning service in this church by quoting these words: 'Now unto him that is able to keep you from falling, and to present you faultless before the presence of his glory with exceeding joy, to the only wise God our Saviour, be glory and majesty, dominion and power, both now and ever' (Jude 24). He is going to do it. 'So he bringeth them unto their desired haven.' What is that? God. Heaven. Eternal bliss. Men and women delivered and emancipated. Right with God. Enjoying the glory. That is the haven. And he *will* bring us to it. Once he starts he never gives up. Once he comes on board he will never go away. He will always be with you. 'I will never leave thee, nor forsake thee.'

It is not surprising that we read that they are 'glad because they be quiet,' and that they rejoice. It is the characteristic of the Christian's life. It does not mean that things will not go wrong outside him or within him, but it does mean that he will never know that desperation again. Even at its worst, he will have a calm and a peace of which the world can never rob him. He has a joy which the world can neither give nor ever take away.

Shall I end by asking you a question? Can you say something like this:

> *When peace, like a river, attendeth my way,*
> *When sorrows, like sea-billows, roll,*
> *Whatever my lot, Thou hast taught me to say,*
> *It is well, it is well, with my soul.*
>
> Horatio Gates Spafford

The man who wrote that had terrible sorrows. Four of his daughters were drowned in mid-Atlantic, and he lost his money in a bank crash. Everything had gone. But, in spite of it, though he was in the midst of a hurricane, he was able to write those words. 'He maketh the storm a calm, so that the waves thereof are still. Then are they glad because they be quiet.'

What of it, my dear friend? How do you feel? Where have you found yourself in life in this world? Are you in the midst of a storm? Are the billows of passion and lust and desire and jealousy and anger—are they buffeting and battering you and shaking you, so that you are like a drunken man staggering through this world? Are you the victim of the next temptation that meets you round any corner that you may chance to turn? Do your life and your happiness depend upon the people whom you meet or whom you do not meet?

Are you a victim of circumstance and chance, or are you enjoying quiet and peace? Do you know where you are going? Is the compass still working? Is the steering gear still in order? Do you see the haven? Are you going steadily in its direction? Do you know where you are? This is an urgent question; you do not know how much longer you will live, so it is about time you knew the answer. Are you going to end in the haven? If the honest answer you must give to that question is that you do not know and that you are afraid, and that the billows are in control of you and you do not know where you are going, well, you must just do this: you must cry out to him and say this to him:

> *Jesu, Lover of my soul,*
> *Let me to Thy bosom fly,*
> *While the nearer waters roll,*
> *While the tempest still is high:*
> *Hide me, O my Saviour hide,*
> *Till the storm of life be past;*
> *Safe into the haven guide;*
> *O receive my soul at last!*

Ask him. Plead with him. Cry out to him in those words and he will receive you, and you will end by saying:

Thou, O Christ, art all I want;
More than all in Thee I find;
Raise the fallen, cheer the faint,
Heal the sick, and lead the blind.

Yes, go on:

Plenteous grace with Thee is found,
Grace to cover all my sin;
Let the healing streams abound,
Make and keep me pure within:
Thou of life the fountain art,
Freely let me take of Thee;
Spring Thou up within my heart,
Rise to all eternity.

Charles Wesley

Cry out unto him in the midst of the ocean, in your agony and despair, and he will deliver you out of your distresses.

Blessed be the name of God; the God of glory who so loved us that, in spite of our sin and folly and shame, he has sent his only Son to pilot us through the voyage and to bring us to the eternal haven.

6
The God of the Bible

He turneth rivers into a wilderness, and the
watersprings into dry ground; a fruitful land into
barrenness, for the wickedness of them that dwell therein.
He turneth the wilderness into a standing water, and dry
ground into watersprings. And there he maketh the hungry to
dwell, that they may prepare a city for habitation; and sow the
fields, and plant vineyards, which may yield fruits of increase.
He blesseth them also, so that they are multiplied greatly; and
suffereth not their cattle to decrease. Again, they are minished
and brought low through oppression, affliction, and sorrow. He
poureth contempt upon princes, and causeth them to wander in
the wilderness, where there is no way. Yet setteth he the poor on
high from affliction, and maketh him families like a flock. The
righteous shall see it, and rejoice: and all iniquity shall
stop her mouth. Whoso is wise, and will observe
these things, even they shall understand the
lovingkindness of the LORD.
(Psalm 107:33-43)

We have considered the Psalmist's four pictures, and that has brought us to the end of the thirty-second verse. But, you notice, the psalm does not stop there but continues with verses 33 to 43. So why does he go on? Why did he not stop when he had finished with his pictures?

Well, this is, again, a part of the essential structure of the psalm. Like all the psalmists, he was not simply writing for our delectation or interest. These men were servants of God; they were preachers. They had been given the poetic gift, so they expressed their teaching in this particular form; but they were not poets primarily. Their interest was not in the art as such. No, as we have seen, the psalmists were out to teach people and to convey a message. They were evangelists, so that they always took great care that all they had been saying was brought to a point and to a focus, and that it was applied.

So this man does precisely that, and in this concluding portion he not only brings his own poem to an end—and from the architectonic point of view produces this perfect symmetry—he also completes his message; he brings us to the point at which he is anxious to arrive. In other words, I suggest that he seems to be asking a question and his question is this: 'Do you see the point of all I have been saying? Have you been so interested in my pictures that you have missed the point of them? Have you been so captivated by my art and by my dramatic powers that you have just been talking to one another and thinking to yourselves about the drama and the picture and the excitement? Have you seen the *message*?' he seems to ask. 'Have you really seen what I am out to convey? Because if you haven't, then my labour is in vain.'

But he is not going to take any risks with us. Like the good teacher that he is—and it is so characteristic of the Bible and the biblical method everywhere—he takes out the lessons for us himself. He says, 'This is what I am teaching.' He underlines it, and then, having extracted the principles out of his own teaching, as he states them here from verses 33 to 42, he concludes with a final word of appeal and says, 'Whoso is wise, and will observe these things, even they [they are the people who] shall understand the lovingkindness of the LORD.' That is his method. That is the analysis of the psalm, which puts into context this final portion, so that we can see exactly what the Psalmist is inviting us to do.

The Bible

Let me put it to you, therefore, like this. This Book, which we call the Bible, is God's Book of Life. I have been reminding you that in it we have incomparable poetry. But we could equally say that we have marvellous history in it. There are all sorts of themes and subjects in the Bible. But it is not an encyclopaedia. It is the 'textbook of life'. It is the 'manual of the soul'. It has one great message. And that message is life and how life is to be lived, how life is to be enjoyed, the object and the purpose of life and the way to live it. That is its only theme. And you find it in this psalm as you find it everywhere else in the Bible.

Here we are, all of us, in this life and in this world. Now the very fact, I take it, that we are considering all this at this moment is proof in and of itself that to us this is something to be contemplated, something to be meditated upon. We are not content—as so many are—just to take things as they come, and never to stand apart for a moment to look at life and at ourselves and to say, 'Here I am in this world, but what is its meaning? What is its purpose?' And then you go on to say to yourself, 'I not only know that I am in this life, I also know that I am only here once. I am here at this moment and, in a sense, I am doing something that I shall never do again.' So life is a tremendous thing.

Now every thoughtful person arrives at some such conclusion and they begin to look at life and at themselves in that kind of context and in that sort of way. Not only that, they have lived long enough to know that in this life and world, certain things happen to us. We saw that very clearly in the picture of the storm at sea. The Bible is full of it. Life brings its problems. It brings its emergencies and its trials. So we begin to experience them and we begin to know something about them, and anxieties and worry tend to follow in their wake. And, as we know, things happen to us from the outside. Here we are at this moment in history. We are aware of certain powers and forces in life and in the world and, of course, they affect us; because though we are just small units, as it were, and, in a sense, the great world seems to be quite indifferent to us, we know that everything that happens in it will affect us. So that we cannot say, 'Ah well, that is an international problem; it has nothing to do with me.' Of course it has everything to do with me! If a war comes I am affected. All our relationships are immediately involved and disturbed.

So we are passing through a world like that with those conditions, and the thoughtful person stops and pauses and considers it and says, 'What is all this? Is there any reason, any explanation of it all? What am I to do about it? How am I to get through it? How can I keep on my feet, as it were, and refuse to be knocked down? How can I stand up and not be submerged and drawn into that vortex and just be carried along without knowing what is happening to me?'

Now the thoughtful people, from the commencement of human history, have stood up like that, and have asked their questions. And the thing they have always asked is this, Where is wisdom? Job, in his poetic way, asks, 'Where shall wisdom be found?' (Job 28:12).That is the question. 'I know where precious metals are to be found. I know where I can get coal; I know where I can get gold; I know where silver is to be mined. These things I know,' says Job, 'but the question is, Where is wisdom?' It has been the great quest, the great endeavour, the great cry of mankind from the dawn of history down until now.

And it is precisely to answer that question that the Psalmist wrote this hundred and seventh psalm. As I told you, he did not write simply in order to paint his wonderful pictures, and to have the marvellous satisfaction of the artist of having produced an amazing artistic work. He did not write all this in order that it might be put up in some sort of gallery and then, when we have nothing better to do, we pay our pound and just go round and look at and admire the amazing art which is displayed. Not at all! He is a man who knew something of the buffetings of life—'The slings and arrows of outrageous fortune', as Shakespeare puts it. And it is because, in the goodness and the mercy of God, the Psalmist has been led to true wisdom, that he passes it on to us. He says, 'I discovered it, I know', and he wants us to know, so he prepares his message. He says, 'Whoso is wise, and will observe these things . . .', having done so, he shall begin to enjoy and to 'understand' and to experience 'the lovingkindness of the LORD' (v.43).

His message

So what is his message? I shall summarise it for you. He still continues to express it in his pictorial manner and, in doing that, he emphasises the principles that he has extracted. Let me extract them still more, and underline them as I am enabled to do. Here, he says, is wisdom. This is the key to the whole understanding of the problem of life and of living.

Relationship with God

In the first place, he says that nothing matters eventually, save our relationship to God. Now that is something that the Bible says in a thousand and one places. It is the great theme and a particularly favourite theme in the Book of Psalms. It is put there, generally, quite boldly like this: 'The fear of the LORD is the beginning of wisdom' (Psalm 111:10). You have not started to be wise until you have realised this. Everything else is the prolegomena, mere introduction. The fear of the Lord is the beginning of wisdom, and the man who does not have the fear of the Lord knows nothing at all about wisdom.

So let us see how this man puts that. Nothing, I repeat, matters, according to the Psalmist here, save our relationship to God. But if you merely look at life superficially and in general, you will not realise that at all, because if you look at life on the surface, as all people do by nature, and as all do who do not realise the vital

107

importance of knowing God, then you take things as they appear. And if you merely do that, you would come to the conclusion that God really has nothing at all to do with it.

And that is exactly where, by nature and as the result of sin, we are all led astray. How do men and women look at life without God? We are given the answer here. People without God look at life and at the world, and they see rivers and watersprings and a fruitful land. But they not only notice those things; they also see that there is something very different. They notice that there are such things as wildernesses and dry and barren ground. Now that is just observation, is it not? And, corresponding to that, you notice that the Psalmist tells us that there are such things in the world as princes. There are some people who are in great power and in great dominion, and they have crowns upon their heads. But, again, they not only notice the princes of this world, they see that there are poor people also.

There, then, are men and women just looking at life, and they say, 'Yes, that is very true of this world and of life. I notice that as I go on a journey in a train or in a motor car, there is a curious variation. I go through the most fertile plains and then I come to a patch of land which is quite barren. I see nothing but some herbs and rushes there. Nothing seems to be growing. There is none of that luscious grass there. And then I go to other places; it is just rock; you can see the rock coming out through the surface; it is valueless, hopeless. I notice, too, as I look at men and women, there seems to be a kind of corresponding variation. Some people are very successful; others never seem to make anything of life. Some are very wealthy and some are very poor. That is life', they say, 'I look at it and I notice that it is characterised by divisions and distinctions based upon heredity or accident or ability; based upon people's industry, ingenuity, zeal, or application, and so on.'

Now those are facts; that is just sheer observation. Yes, but the vital question is, How do you explain all that? What accounts for it?

It is no use denying the facts, but the interesting thing is the explanation of them. How can I become a prince? How can I become a very wealthy man? I do not want to be poor. How can I have this fruitful land, as it were, and become fruitful myself? Those are the great questions. What is the meaning of all this inequality that one sees, and all this variety and variation?

Now the world thinks it has very adequate explanations. Some say it is but accident and chance; there is no rhyme and reason in it at all. Things are what they are and they will be what they will be, and that is it; and that is all they can say. They say there is no design; there is nothing here at all. That is a fatalist—and sometimes he is a scientist, but he is a fatalist. Then there are others who say, as I have indicated, that it can be explained in terms of heredity, perhaps. Or others say it is the law of supply and demand. Others say that it is a whole question of a person's ability and application, and that life is what you make of it. There is, they say, no need to talk about God. A man makes his own bed; he determines his own fate. He really reaps what he himself has sown, and everything is the result of what he himself has done about life in this world.

Those are the attitudes, I think you will agree, of the vast majority of people today. God is not in their thoughts at all. 'The fool hath said in his heart, There is no God' (Psalm 14:1). And they say that there is no God because there is no need of a God. If you can explain the world in terms of science and evolution and development, and if you can explain the whole of history in terms of some dialectic, some economic dialectic, or something like that, and certain laws that you think you can discover, then God is just unnecessary. That is the prevailing attitude and opinion; we do not believe in God today because we know so much that we know that God is not necessary.

But that, according to the Psalmist, as it is the message of the whole Bible, is the very essence of folly. The one thing we can be

109

certain of is that everything is under God and is in God's hands, and that God controls everything. 'He turneth rivers into a wilderness, and the watersprings into dry ground; a fruitful land into barrenness, for the wickedness of them that dwell therein.' And on the other hand, 'He turneth the wilderness into a standing water, and dry ground into watersprings. And there he maketh the hungry to dwell . . . Yet setteth he the poor on high'. He treats the princes with contempt, we are told. He laughs at them, but the same God takes the poor 'and maketh him families like a flock'.

Now, this is the great first article of the Christian faith, as it is the first message of the Bible: it is that God is over all; that 'the LORD reigneth' (Psalm 96:10). 'So', you may say, 'why then are things as they are?' And the answer of the Bible is that we are confronted by the mind of eternal God, which eludes our understanding; but that there is an understanding, there is a purpose, and there is a design. But when we apply our own little canons of thought to it, we are often bewildered and baffled, and God seems to us to be inconsistent simply because of our failure to understand; for we are told this about him, that 'He maketh his sun to rise on the evil and on the good, and sendeth rain on the just and on the unjust' (Matthew 5:45).

God is over all, yes, but he permits certain things. He permits the evil to flourish for a while like the 'green bay tree' (Psalm 37:35). And the fact that that man is flourishing like that does not mean that there is not a God. That is what people argue, is it not? 'Ah,' they say, 'if there is a God, and if God is what you say he is, we could not have the position as we see it. You say that unless a man lives a godly life God is not for him and he will be doomed. But look at the world. Look at the way in which the people who deny God and laugh at him flourish, and look at their great success. Where is your God?' they say. 'Where is your consistency?'

But I have given you the answer of the Bible. God allows rivers to flow, he allows the watersprings to spring up. But it is all under his control; he can revoke it in a second. He does not always do it, but he can; he is over it all. 'The LORD reigneth. Let the people tremble' (Psalm 99:1). So the Bible's first and great fundamental message is that though we do not always understand it, and though we cannot see it very clearly at times, nevertheless, we are all in his hands.

That is the wonderful thing about the Bible, and that is where these historical portions of the Bible are so invaluable. They give us these great panoramic views of history; they take in these great epochs in a great sweep. That is the astounding thing about them; you are standing with God, as it were, when you are reading the Bible, and you are looking down upon the stream of history. But so often, as you look superficially, you say, 'There is no God. Look at what is happening! Look at that great dynasty coming up; look at that mighty empire arising, and look where God's people are!' Ah, but that is only the temporary view. Take a long view; keep on looking and you will see, if you follow it on, that God was there the whole time, and when you decided it was hopeless, in he came, as it were; he irrupted into it all, and all your history seems to be turned upside down.

But let me go on to put that to you in a little more detail. The one thing we must grasp is that the most vital and important thing in the world is our relationship to God.

Truth about God
So the second principle arises, by a logical necessity. It is important for all of us to know the truth about God, and the Bible is a book which is devoted to that theme. That is its message. It is a revelation of God. Yes, that is the great thing: not primarily that you and I may have something, but that we may know him.

The Lord Jesus Christ, the Son of God, came into this world . . . Why, first and foremost? Still the same! 'No man hath seen God at any time; the only begotten Son, which is in the bosom of the

Father, he hath declared him' (John 1:18). 'God, who at sundry times and in divers manners spake in time past unto the fathers by the prophets, hath in these last days spoken unto us by his Son' (Hebrews 1:1,2). Revelation! God revealing the truth about himself to men. Why? Because it is the fundamental, cardinal article in wisdom, and therefore the most important thing for you and for me and for all of us is to know the truth about God. It is infinitely more important than that you should know if there is going to be another war or not; infinitely more important than any other particular subject you may chance to be interested in.

Why is this? I have already given you the reason. You and I are but pilgrims and strangers, travellers and sojourners, here today and gone tomorrow, living our life in this world. We are doing something that we only do once; we will never come back to it again, and our eternal destiny depends upon what we do now. So it is not just a question of how to enjoy life in this world. It is the safeguarding of my eternal future; and it all depends upon my knowledge of God. What is God like? Who is he? How am I to know this God? What is my relationship to him? You have the answer here in this man's pictorial form, and may God give us grace and by his Spirit enable us to receive the truth.

The whole trouble in the world today is due to the fact that men and women have their own ideas of God and do not come to the Bible for it. How constantly one is being told this—I was told it only recently by a friend with whom I was having a conversation and who is concerned about a dear one. 'He says', said the friend, 'that he doesn't understand how a God of love can do this or that.' It is always the same, is it not?

Now I do not have the time to argue it out now, but let me put it to you like this quite simply: What do we really know of God apart from the Bible? Have you ever tried to face that question? What authority have you got for your views? You say this and that; that is your thought, that is your philosophy; and you do not know everything, and your mind, like mine, is not perfect. Yet we base our view of God upon what *we* think God ought to be like. That is essential folly!

No, no, if we are to know anything about God we must come to this book, and we must believe and accept its revelation. You can read your philosophers and you will find that they have never arrived at him; they do not know. They call him 'the ultimate reality', or 'the absolute', or some kind of 'philosophic X'. How does that help us? No, there is no knowledge of God except the knowledge he has given, and this is the record of what he has given. This is the revelation. And, above all, you see it in his dear Son who came from heaven in order to bring it to us.

So what do we know about God? Well, here are the things that are revealed: *God is righteous*. God is just. God is holy. 'God is light, and in him is no darkness at all' (1 John 1:5). Take it if you like in the words of this Psalmist: 'He turneth rivers into a wilderness, and the watersprings into dry ground; a fruitful land into barrenness . . .' Why does he do it? Here is the answer: '. . . for the wickedness of them that dwell therein' (v.34). Wickedness! And later on in the same passage we have this other term *iniquity.* Have we not had it in our four pictures as we have looked at them one by one? Why have all those people got into distress? Is it not always the same thing? 'Fools . . . because of their iniquities' (v.17), because they have 'contemned the counsel of the most High' (v.11). It is because of their rebellion, their arrogance, their sin. Oh, that is but an emphasis of the justice and the righteousness and the holiness of God.

Now the world not only forgets that, it hates it, and the world is as it is today because it does not believe that God is righteous. It wants a God who will just be an agency to dole out blessings and happiness when we need them, and will wink at our sins and say, 'It's all right, I take no notice.' That is the world's idea, and there is nothing that the natural man or woman hates so much as this doctrine

113

of the righteousness and the holiness and the justice of God. But, whether you and I like it or not, the fact is that God is like that. His own dear Son in addressing him always said, 'Holy Father', 'Righteous Father'. God dwells in 'the light which no man can approach unto' (1 Timothy 6:16). A burning light. An eternal light. That is the first thing, therefore, that is emphasised here, and this Psalmist would have us see it. He says, 'Whoso is wise, and will observe these things' (v.43).

The second thing he tells us about God is *his greatness and his power.* It is, too, a great theme of the Bible. 'In the beginning God created the heaven and the earth' (Genesis 1:1). God the creator. God the controller. God the sustainer of everything. This man brings it out with particular force in his poetry. He tells us that there is nothing that God cannot do. He can turn a river into a wilderness. He can turn a waterspring into dry ground. He can take a fruitful land and make it absolutely barren.

'Is anything too hard for the Lord?' 'With God nothing shall be impossible.' As one of our hymns puts it so well, 'He can create and he destroy.' And the Psalmist is anxious that we should see that. He has been showing us in the four pictures of the marvellous deliverances God has given. So how does God do it? Well, he puts it in terms of God's greatness and power. He is the God over all; having made everything, he controls everything. Nothing can exist and go on living apart from God. 'He giveth to all life, and breath, and all things', says the apostle Paul to the Athenians (Acts 17:25), and if he withdraws that breath, says Psalm 104, everything would collapse in a second (v.29). The whole creation is in the hand of God.

Even the scientists are beginning to speak like that. The more they understand of the nature of an atom, the more convinced they are of this very thing. Everything is being held, as it were, in this tremendous movement, in this great tension. There is energy at the back of it all. Where does that come from? God! God at the back of it all, organising, sustaining; the creator, the artificer; the sustainer of everything that is.

That is the Psalmist's message. And if you read these verses—as I plead with you to do—watch his description of what God can do. He can tumble things upside down. That mighty river can suddenly disappear, and that barrenness can spring up with water. It can become a great lake, a standing pool. Why? It is the creator who is doing it all. There is no limit to his greatness and to his power.

I like these psalms! I like these psalmists! This Psalmist has been speaking about nature, but listen to him saying it about human beings. Listen to this: 'He poureth contempt upon princes, and causeth them to wander in the wilderness, where there is no way' (v.40). 'There is no respect of persons with God' (Romans 2:11). There are no class and social distinctions where God is concerned. There are no VIPs in the eyes of the Almighty. There is no priority where he is concerned. 'He poureth contempt upon princes' if they do not acknowledge him and submit to him.

> *Princes and lords may flourish, or may fade;*
> *A breath can make them, as a breath has made.*
>   Oliver Goldsmith

Yes, this great God is a God like that. His greatness, his majesty, and his power—history is full of this. Read the Old Testament. The trouble with men and women today is that they do not read, and they do not know their Old Testament. If you want to see God pouring his contempt upon princes, then read the accounts given there of the great dynasties that arose. Look at Egypt rising and striding the world as a colossus, and then God poured his contempt upon her and down she went; Pharaoh and his hosts overwhelmed in the Red Sea, a laughing stock to the nations.

Then do you remember how he reduced a man like Nebuchadnezzar almost to the condition of an ox? Nebuchadnezzar stood up and said that he was a god and that men must worship him. And God poured his contempt upon him, so he was out in the fields and his hair grew and his nails grew like talons, and there he was, eating grass like an ox. 'He poureth contempt upon princes.'

There is a most notable case also in the New Testament: in the twelfth chapter of the Book of the Acts of the Apostles. A king called Herod sat upon the throne in his royal apparel, delivering a great oration, and the people cried out saying, 'It is the voice of a god, and not of a man.' And he allowed them to say so. But not for long, because God sent an angel who smote him and he was consumed with worms and 'gave up the ghost'. 'He poureth contempt upon princes.'

That is the God whom the Bible reveals. The mightiest emperors and princes of Nineveh and of Greece and of any other country that has ever been, unless they acknowledge him, he will pour contempt upon them, and they vanish out of sight.

The next thing that the Bible tells us about him is *the absolute certainty of judgement*. This God who is righteous and holy and just, and who is so mighty and powerful, is a God who is going to judge the world. Oh, I know that this is the height of unpopularity. It is the thing that modern men and women absolutely hate because, if they did not, they would be like their forefathers of a hundred years ago who could be frightened by a sermon like this. But modern people? Of course not! They know so much; they are so scientific. But the facts are still exactly the same, and all that this man is saying here is being proved and exemplified in the modern world at this very hour. God is going to judge. Here it is once more: 'He turneth rivers into a wilderness, and the watersprings into dry ground; a fruitful land into barrenness, for the wickedness of them that dwell therein' (vv.33-34).

I say it with reverence: God judges because he is God. He must. His holy nature insists upon it. And not only that, he has told us that he will judge. When he made the man and the woman at the

116

beginning, he told them quite plainly, 'If you live like this I will bless you; but if you break my commandments, I will judge you.' And the Old Testament is nothing but a record of this. It began in Eden. Though Adam and Eve were made in the image of God, when they sinned, God judged them, and he turned them out of the Garden and prevented their return. That is the Bible. That is the gospel. That is an essential part of preaching Jesus Christ: that men and women in estrangement from God are under the wrath of God. Not only would Jesus Christ never have come but for that, he would not have been needed but for that.

The story of Eden is the story of judgement. Go on and read the story of the Flood. Read about Sodom and Gomorrah. Read about Jerusalem, the city of God himself, his chosen people, being attacked and sacked by the Chaldeans and reduced to a mass of rubble.

It is judgement, and it does not matter who they are. If it is his own people, if it is the man of his own choice, it does not matter. Look at David, a favourite with God; but he sins and God punishes him. It is the law of God. It is absolute. It is eternal. And then, hurry along to AD 70 when the Jewish nation, having rejected her own Messiah in the very person of the only begotten Son of God, was again surrounded by the Roman legionaries and sacked and destroyed, and the Temple smashed, and the nation thrown out amongst the other nations, where they remain until today.

What is it? It is judgement. History is full of it. Read the Old Testament history again and compare it with secular history. Look at it in subsequent history. Nations rising with great pomp and apparently controlling the whole world. They come up one after another, Napoleons of various types, but the time comes when they are struck, and they vanish and they are gone.

There seem to be powers and authorities and mights in the world today that cause us to tremble. In a sense it is right that we should do so, but as I look at them all in the light of this psalm and the teaching of the Bible, there is a sense in which I almost tremble for them. In the hands of God they are but as grasshoppers. We read about their wealth, their armaments—this country, other countries, I do not care which you are thinking of. Think of them all together: all national power, all human government, is against God. It is the beast of the book of Revelation. And it does not matter whether we belong to it or not, if it does not acknowledge God, it is under God's judgement. They are but 'as the small dust of the balances' to him (Isaiah 40:15), and they will all come to judgement.

But I am not only speaking about nations. I am speaking about individuals. The same thing is true. 'Though the mills of God grind slowly, yet they grind exceeding small' (F. von Logau; trans. Longfellow). Ah, says someone, it is all very well to preach like that. People have been preaching like that for centuries, but the world has gone on. I know. Peter has already answered that objection in the third chapter of his second Epistle. He says men do not understand that 'one day is with the Lord as a thousand years, and a thousand years as one day' (2 Peter 3:8). That is what makes preaching such a terrible thing, such a responsible thing; and God forbid that I should do it unworthily or come between anybody and this message. But the message is that you are face to face with God and he will judge you by what he has told you in the Bible. You were meant for him and you are meant to glorify him, and if you do not you are under the wrath of God, and a day will come when you will know it.

Do not be deluded by the fact that, so far, things may have gone well with you. That though you have turned your back against God and have laughed at him and have gone your own way, you have done well, you have made money and everything is going well. O my dear friend, do not be a fool! Do not take that ridiculous short view. Read the Old Testament history and see yourself. Judgement will come. We must all meet him and stand before him. Judgement!

And, lastly, I thank God that I can end with this: the final thing we are told about God is *his loving kindness.* 'Whoso is wise, and will observe these things, even they shall understand the loving-kindness of the LORD' (v.43). Judgement first, yes. Repentance first, obviously. John the Baptist first. But, thank God, he is only the forerunner of the Lord Jesus Christ. God is holy and righteous and just and pure. His might, his majesty, his power are illimitable, and he will judge the world in righteousness. But, thank God, God is love also. God is full of loving kindness and compassion and tender mercy. And as we have seen in our four amazing pictures, when we are reduced to the end and are in our distress and are desperate and know not what to do in the storms of life, and we cry out unto him, the answer is already there even before we have made our request. 'God so loved the world, that he gave his only begotten Son, that whosoever believeth in him should not perish, but have everlasting life' (John 3:16).

I have kept you with this aspect in this sermon because you cannot deal with the two sides in one sermon. Next, God willing, I hope to elaborate the other side and show this amazing loving kindness of God. But no one will ever know that until they realise the truth about God. People say to me, 'Why do you talk about the blood of Christ?' They have never seen any need for it. Why? Because they have never known what sin is. They have never known God. They have no conception of his glory, his holiness, his majesty, his righteousness. They have never seen him. They have never seen themselves. If they had, they would be desperate and they would thank God for Christ.

So we have been looking through this blessed revelation that God has been pleased to give us; at God himself; and ourselves in the sight of God. But there is a hope that I may be preaching to somebody who may be dead before a week tonight. It may be your last opportunity, so I do not let you go without saying this. My friend, if you have seen the truth, Christ has died for you and your sins can be forgiven, and the moment you believe, they are. The loving kindness of the Lord! But if God spares me and spares you until next Sunday night, come back and I will tell you something about that loving kindness.

The God who turns the rivers into a wilderness is the same God who can turn a wilderness into a spring, into a fountain. That is the gospel in all its glory and its fulness.

Do you know God? Do you know your relationship to God? It determines the character and the nature of your life in this world. It determines whether in eternity you will enjoy everlasting bliss or eternal misery.

7
The salvation of God

*'He turneth rivers into a wilderness, and the
watersprings into dry ground; a fruitful land into
barrenness, for the wickedness of them that dwell
therein. He turneth the wilderness into a standing water,
and dry ground into watersprings. And there he maketh the
hungry to dwell, that they may prepare a city for habitation;
and sow the fields, and plant vineyards, which may yield fruits
of increase. He blesseth them also, so that they are multiplied
greatly; and suffereth not their cattle to decrease. Again, they
are minished and brought low through oppression, affliction, and
sorrow. He poureth contempt upon princes, and causeth them to
wander in the wilderness, where there is no way. Yet setteth he the
poor on high from affliction, and maketh him families like a flock.
The righteous shall see it, and rejoice: and all iniquity shall stop
her mouth. Whoso is wise, and will observe these things, even
they shall understand the lovingkindness of the LORD.'*
(Psalm 107:33-43)

Christian preaching always confronts men and women with the biggest and the greatest and the most important thing in life. There are probably meetings being held in this country and in other countries at this moment to consider other matters, and they are all of importance. Alas, there are some holding political meetings tonight, and they are considering the present world crisis, the present situation. There are others who are met together to have cultural discussions about art and literature and music. There are things like that and, again, they have their importance. They should not be doing such things on a Sunday—though that is not my point at the moment—but they do these things on weekdays also.

But the whole message of the Bible is that while all those things have their place and their importance, there is nothing which compares in importance with this—a man or woman's relationship to God. Because, after this world has gone and has passed away, we shall still be face to face with God. Whether there is a war, or whether there is not, whether an international arrangement and agreement are possible or not; still the soul remains and God remains and there we are, face to face with him. In life in this world, nothing matters but our relationship to God.

So it follows from that, obviously, that the next important thing is that we should know the truth about God. If the biggest thing for me is my relationship to God, then I want to know the truth about him. And here the Psalmist tells us about it. We have considered one aspect of it, which is that God is righteous, and just, and holy, and that there is no end to his might and to his power. God is the judge eternal, whom no one can evade and no one can escape; the judge of all the earth, God the almighty.

Salvation

So the Psalmist's object is to enlighten us about these things; but, thank God, he does not stop there. He then goes on to tell us something about God as our saviour—the salvation of God. Did you notice the alternation in this last passage—first one side, then the other? God's salvation first. He began by saying, 'Oh that men would praise the LORD for his goodness' (v.31). But why don't they? Well, generally, because they do not understand this salvation of his.

And that is really the ultimate explanation of why anybody in the world is not a Christian. They just do not know and they do not understand God's way of salvation. It is because somewhere or another they have got wrong ideas about this; they have never understood it. If only they knew it, if only they believed it and began to experience it, they would rejoice in it. That is why the Psalmist gives his invitation. 'O give thanks', he says, 'unto the LORD, for he is good: for his mercy endureth for ever.'

Did you know that? I ask again, are you praising God? Are you thanking him? Is there a song of praise and of thanksgiving in your heart? Are you ready to join this man's great choir that he is assembling together from the east and from the west, from the north and from the south, to sing the praises of God? Or do you say, 'I am not conscious of a sense of praise and of thanksgiving. I don't want to thank God; I don't see any reason for thanking him. I am finding life very difficult and the world very difficult. Thanking God! My attitude is this: if there is a God, well, why are things as they are? And why is he allowing things to be as they are? I cannot praise God. I am not conscious of his goodness.' Now if that is the position, it is because somewhere or another you do not understand God's way of salvation and you have got wrong ideas about it.

So let us get our minds disabused of these erroneous conceptions and look at it as it is unfolded and expounded to us by the Psalmist in this concluding section of Psalm 107. What are the characteristics of this salvation that God gives to men and women?

Reversal
The first thing is that it is a complete reversal of all our natural ideas. I always like to start with that principle as I preach this gospel. The gospel of our Lord and Saviour Jesus Christ reverses all our human, our natural ideas. It turns them literally upside down. There is nothing else in the world like it.

Now there are many people who obviously do not agree with that, because they betray themselves in the things they say. They talk about 'great religious teachers' and 'great religious geniuses'. They bring out their lists. They talk about Moses and Jeremiah, and they talk about Buddha, and Confucius, and the Christ, and others. And by saying that, they are at once telling us that they have never understood the first thing about the Christian way of salvation, which is its uniqueness. It is not a philosophy in series with a whole host of other philosophies, nor is it just a teaching like others. It is entirely different and it is entirely on its own.

This is how the Psalmist puts it: 'He turneth the wilderness into a standing water, and dry ground into watersprings' (v.35). Is that the sort of thing we find happening in this world? Do you suddenly turn around a corner and find a wilderness becoming standing water and dry barren ground suddenly springing up? 'Ah,' says somebody, 'life is not like that, you know. You get that sort of thing in the fairy tales and in the fantasies, but that is not life. Life is hard; it is a grind; it is cruel, and you do not suddenly get these amazing reversals and surprises.' That is the natural man or woman's thinking about God's way of salvation.

But the whole of the New Testament gives us the exact opposite impression. It starts like this. A priest goes into the temple to do his duty and suddenly he sees an angel. He is not expecting it, but there an angel suddenly appears and says to him, 'Zacharias, you and your wife Elisabeth are going to have a child.' 'It is impossible!' says the man. 'Don't you know how old we are? This thing cannot take place.' But that was the announcement, and it did take place. And so it continues. Do you remember the angel going to Mary and talking to her about that 'holy thing' that would be born out of her? She says, 'How can this thing be? I have never known a man.' Nevertheless, it was to be and it did happen.

You see, we are in a realm which is altogether different. It is not like anything else. This is what the Christian gospel claims, and the tragedy is that we all start with the other idea and the other prejudice, that Christianity is just a higher form of morality, a morality 'touched with emotion' as Matthew Arnold put it. We say that it really depends upon what we do, and so on, and we are not expecting this kind of thing. But this is the gospel; the reversal of all our thinking and all our ideas.

Then, secondly, because of that, the gospel is quite surprising. Indeed, I will go further and say that it is quite incredible to the natural man. You read this psalm and you say that that, of course, is typical of the poets with their imagery and their hyperbole, their vivid imaginations. They like playing with ideas, but it is all poetry. But this is not poetry; this is fact!

You find the apostle Paul putting this in his own particular way in his various epistles in the New Testament. He says, 'The natural man receiveth not the things of the Spirit of God: for they are foolishness unto him' (1 Corinthians 2:14). When the Greeks were confronted with this gospel, they laughed at it, they dismissed it. They said, 'Fancy asking us to believe something like that! That a carpenter—in a little land like Palestine, of all places—is the Saviour, and that he saves not by propounding a great new philosophic system, but by being crucified in utter weakness upon a cross on a hill called Calvary! Rubbish and nonsense! Sheer folly!' That is what they said; and they said it because it was such a reversal of all they had ever thought and imagined.

But the gospel of Jesus Christ is surprising, and if it does not come to us as a surprise, we have really never known it. Indeed, if you have never felt about the gospel that there is something almost incredible about it, you do not have the real thing. It is something that is a counter to human ideas and appears to be utter fancy and fantasy and foolishness.

Demands nothing

So in what particular respects does this gospel reverse all our ideas? In what respects does it come as a surprise or seem to be almost incredible to us? The first is that *it demands nothing of us*. Nothing whatsoever! The Psalmist says, 'He turneth the wilderness into a standing water'. Men and women by nature are but as the wilderness. 'He turneth . . . dry ground into watersprings.' By nature they are nothing but dry ground. 'There he maketh the hungry to dwell.' By nature they are hungry. 'That they may prepare a city for habitation.' They have no certain and secure dwelling; and so on. And the Psalmist repeats this later on. Having said that 'He poureth contempt upon princes, and causeth them to wander in the wilderness, where there is no way', he goes on to say, 'Yet setteth he the poor on high from affliction, and maketh him families like a flock.'

My first principle, therefore, is that the gospel—this way of salvation—demands nothing of us at all. It tells us that we are in a state of barrenness, we are as dry ground, a wilderness, and we are in a state of extreme poverty.

That is the New Testament doctrine. The New Testament comes to us and tells us that we are born into the world in a state of sin, and that we aggravate it and increase it and bring ourselves to this condition of complete barrenness, spiritual barrenness, spiritual poverty. It tells us that we are penniless and helpless and that we have nothing whatsoever.

Now if you do not agree with that, let me prove it to you. Would you like to know how much you have by way of spiritual possession? Well, test yourself by this: 'Thou shalt love the Lord thy God with all thy heart, and with all thy soul, and with all thy strength, and with all thy mind; and thy neighbour as thyself' (Luke 10:27). Are we doing that? That is the way to test this yourself. Then, test yourself in terms of love, joy, peace, longsuffering, goodness, meekness, gentleness, faith, temperance. How much of these fruits do we possess and are we producing? That is the way to face it.

So the Bible tells us that we are in this state of barrenness, but—and this is the astounding thing—it also tells us that this makes no difference at all. God demands nothing of us but the recognition of that. He does not demand goodness of us, nor does he demand morality or works. He does not demand of us right ideas and wonderful conceptions of life and understanding. He makes no such demand at all. And the wonderful thing is that our lack of these things and our extreme poverty are no hindrance whatsoever.

But this, surely, is the very point at which we all, by nature, tend to go astray. We all tend to think that becoming a Christian and sharing in the Christian salvation is something that is the result of our goodness, or our morality, or our working, or fasting, or praying, or sweating, or something like that. We say, 'I am going to make myself a Christian. By my own efforts I am going to make myself a good man or woman.' But the gospel confronts us with the exact opposite. It says, 'All our righteousnesses are as filthy rags' (Isaiah 64:6). All the things of which even a Saul of Tarsus can boast are nothing but dung and loss and refuse (Philippians 3:8). So the man who thinks himself the most wealthy, when he confronts this, is proved to be a pauper. He has nothing at all: wilderness, barrenness, extreme poverty and helplessness.

And the glorious thing about this salvation is that, far from telling us that because we are like that we are hopeless, it tells us, in a sense, that that is the very condition to receiving the salvation. Did you notice how the Psalmist's four pictures brought out this point? These four people he depicts, these types of persons, end by praising God. So what was it that led them to praise him? Was it not this? that 'they cried unto the LORD in their trouble, and he delivered them out of their distresses.' They did nothing at all but cry out. It was not that they had made some superhuman effort and had at last extricated themselves out of their troubles. They could not! The wanderers in the wilderness could not find the way; the man in the prison cell could not break the bars of iron and smash the gates of brass; the man dying on the sick bed could not suddenly rejuvenate and revivify himself; and no human being can quell a storm at sea. No, no, they were utterly, absolutely helpless. All they did was to cry out in their distress.

That is the Old Testament way of putting it, but do you

remember how Christ himself, our blessed Lord and Saviour, puts it? He says, 'I am not come to call the righteous, but sinners to repentance' (Matthew 9:13). 'They that be whole need not a physician, but they that are sick' (Matthew 9:12). He was the 'friend of publicans and sinners' (Luke 7:34). His whole trouble, indeed, was with people like the Pharisees who said, 'No, no, you are wrong. What makes a man right with God is his own efforts and striving, and it is our righteousness that will put us right with God.' But our Lord was saying the exact opposite, and they so hated him for saying it that they crucified him.

But it is the essence of the gospel message. We, with our high ideas of ourselves and of our abilities, believe that we have it in us even to put ourselves right with God. We think that our efforts and our moralities will be enough, and that we really can raise ourselves up. The gospel replies by saying, 'You are a wilderness, a barrenness, a dry ground and a pauper.' But the marvellous thing about it is that that is the very condition of salvation. A hymn puts this very well:

> *All the fitness He requireth*
> *Is to feel your need of Him.*
> Joseph Hart

Nothing else at all. The condition in which God likes to see people coming is this: he likes to see people coming who say,

> *Nothing in my hand I bring,*
> *Simply to Thy cross I cling;*
> *Naked, come to Thee for dress;*
> *Helpless, look to Thee for grace;*
> *Foul, I to the fountain fly;*
> *Wash me, Saviour, or I die.*
> Augustus Toplady

Or,

> *Just as I am, without one plea* [—nothing at all]
> *But that Thy blood was shed for me . . .*
>   Charlotte Elliott

Am I making it plain? Do you not see that this is a reversal of everything that people think and expect? People like to think of Jesus Christ as just the greatest teacher the world has ever known, and the greatest moral exemplar; and their idea of salvation is that, having read the New Testament, or having listened to expositions of it, having got a picture of Christ in their minds, they then say, 'Now, I am going to be like him—*The Imitation of Christ*. I am going to follow him. I shall make great sacrifices; I will give up money or a great post; I will go to the heart of Africa; I will do this, or that, and I will be like him. I am doing it!'

But it is an utter denial of the gospel. The glory of the gospel is this: that you and I not only *can* do nothing, we are not *expected* to do anything. He asks nothing of anyone but just this: that you see yourself as you are in the sight of God. That you recognise your sin, your emptiness and your woe. That you visualise yourself on your death bed; that you visualise yourself on the dread day of judgement, standing before God, with the law being put up against you, and the Sermon on the Mount, and the saints, and Christ himself—and you having to say that you conformed to that! It just means that having faced that, you say, 'I am a sinner. I don't know God; I haven't loved God; I haven't served him. I have lived to myself. I have been selfish. I have done things though I knew they were wrong.'

That is what he asks of us. That we see our need, our barrenness, our wilderness condition, and that we confess it and acknowledge it; that we go to him and say, 'I have no defence, I have no plea of mitigation to offer. I have nothing to say except this: have mercy upon me!' Repentance: that is all he demands.

Complete dependence

The *second* respect in which the gospel is the reversal of everything that we have ever thought follows naturally from the first.
Salvation, as it makes no demands on us, *depends entirely and only
on what God does, what God has done*. The Psalmist says,

> *He* turneth rivers into a wilderness, and the watersprings into dry
> ground . . . *He* turneth the wilderness into a standing water, and
> dry ground into watersprings. And there *he* maketh the hungry
> to dwell, that they may prepare a city for habitation . . . *He* bles-
> seth them also, so that they are multiplied greatly . . . Again, they
> are minished and brought low . . . *He* poureth contempt upon
> princes . . . Yet setteth *he* the poor on high from affliction, and
> maketh him families like a flock.

It is God all along, and you see this everywhere in the Scriptures. You cannot get away from it. Listen to Paul putting it in his
own words: 'I am not ashamed', he says, 'of the gospel of Christ'.
Why? Well, here is the answer: 'It is the power of God unto salvation to everyone that believeth' (Romans 1:16).

It is what *God* is doing. It is a righteousness from God. The
essence of salvation is what God has done in Christ. 'Christ crucified . . .', says Paul, is 'the wisdom of God' (1 Corinthians 1:23-24).
And he is the power of God. Paul also says, 'For after that in the
wisdom of God the world by wisdom knew not God, it pleased
God by the foolishness of preaching to save them that believe' (1
Corinthians 1:21). The world by wisdom knew not God. Plato had
lived, and so had Socrates and Aristotle. The great philosophers
had all lived and they had all tried to find him, but they could not.
'The world by wisdom knew not God.' Man had done his utmost,
his everything, but he could not get there. And when that had come
to pass, 'it pleased God by the foolishness of preaching'—the foolishness of the thing preached—'to save them that believe'.

And Paul works this out and shows how God reverses the whole conception of men and women and turns all our systems completely upside down in every respect and to every degree. He tells us that God has made foolish the wisdom of men. In that same chapter, he says, 'But God hath chosen the foolish things of the world to confound the wise; and God hath chosen the weak things of the world to confound the things which are mighty; and base things of the world, and things which are despised, hath God chosen, yea, and things which are not, to bring to nought things that are' (1 Corinthians 1:27-28). That is the gospel.

Then again, in 2 Corinthians 5 Paul says, God has committed to me this gospel, this message of reconciliation. What is it? 'To wit, that God was in Christ, reconciling the world unto himself, not imputing their trespasses unto them' (v.19). It is *God* doing it. It is *God's* action. We start with this opposite idea that we must do something and the answer is, No, no; God does it! Who can turn a wilderness into standing water but God? Who can turn this dry ground into watersprings but the Lord God Almighty? But he has done it. And he has done it in and through our Lord and Saviour Jesus Christ.

And that is the very essence of the gospel message. It is portrayed before us in the Communion Service by means of bread and of wine, which represent the broken body and the shed blood of the only begotten Son of God. That is how God does it. He sent him into the world; the incarnation is God's action. He sent his Son and prepared him a body. It was a miracle. The Holy Ghost came upon Mary; it was a virgin birth. That was God's way of doing it. He has done it in this person, and he has even gone to the extent of 'laying upon him the iniquity of us all' (Isaiah 53:6). He has put your sins and mine and our guilt upon the person of his only begotten Son. 'He hath made him to be sin for us, who knew no sin; that we might be made the righteousness of God in him' (2 Corinthians 5:21). It is God's action.

Look at Calvary and there you see it. What is happening there? Oh, it is not merely that certain cruel men have condemned the Son of God to death. The Pharisees and scribes and the Roman power were but the human instruments. That is not what is happening there. Calvary is not just a human tragedy. It is not just that men have done a certain thing. No, no! It is an eternal action. It is something that God is doing. God has 'made him to be sin for us'. He has 'laid on him the iniquity of us all'. 'With his stripes we are healed' (Isaiah 53:5,6). And the Son was taking our sins upon himself in his own body on the tree. That is what is happening there. It is God. '*He* turneth the wilderness into a standing water, and dry ground into watersprings' (v.35). All along, from beginning to end, it is this mighty action of God.

Very well then, that comes to us in a practical way like this. You and I have no need to do anything in order to have this great salvation. The Son of God has done it all. Salvation is a free gift. It is not a programme which we are set on in order to earn forgiveness. God forgives us for one reason only, and that is that he has punished our sins in the person of his own Son. It is not our pleading. It is not our repentance. It is not our works. Salvation is a free gift. That is why you can receive it now at any moment. That is why you need never wait or tarry. It is no use saying, 'Well now, I am rather interested in this. I can see that I am a sinner, and I want to go to heaven, I want to be a Christian. I am going to decide, therefore, that I will . . .' Not at all, my friend! The moment you say that, you have gone wrong. You just come as a pauper, and you receive the free gift of God.

It was all done nearly two thousand long years ago in that amazing transaction on the cross on Calvary's hill. The perfect, complete, full salvation was prepared there, because I hear the Son of God saying—have you heard him saying it?—'It is finished.' Everything that was necessary to save you and me—I mean by that, to get rid of our guilt, to blot out our sins, to reconcile us to God, to make us children of God—everything that was necessary for that was done there. It has all been done. It was done before you were ever born into this world. There is nothing left for you to do except to believe and to see that it was done there and to receive the free gift of salvation. You see what a complete reversal it is of everything we have ever thought. But this is God's way. This is the Christian salvation.

This is what Martin Luther came to see. He became the man he was simply because he saw one thing, and it was this very thing to which I have been calling your attention. There was that excellent young man who wanted to be godly, that young man who wanted to know God; so he became a monk. And you look at him in his cell: there he was fasting, believing that that would help him; doing good deeds and giving alms; studying the Scriptures; trying to perfect himself; trying to put himself right with God; taking his sacraments, believing, as his church had taught him, that grace came materially in and through the sacraments, that as he ate that bread he was eating the very body of the Son of God. He believed that all this would put grace into him mechanically, inject it into him as it were. He was doing all these things, and yet he remained miserable and unhappy and sad and ill at ease.

He followed all the other methods. But you remember the story. Suddenly, in reading the Scriptures, he saw how wrong it all was, and this phrase flashed upon his soul, the Holy Spirit opened his mind to see it: 'The just shall live by faith' (Romans 1:17). He saw that he had nothing to do, that it had all been done, that he had but to receive it. Christ had done everything. He need kill himself no more. Christ had been killed and, there, it had come to him as a free gift of God.

And do you remember what happened? He began to sing. He had not been singing before. If you try to fit yourself to meet God you will not have much time for singing. You will be so conscious of failure that you will go the rest of your life mourning. But the moment Luther saw this he began to sing. He began to rejoice. He said, '"Oh that men would praise the LORD for his goodness, and for his wonderful works to the children of men!"(v.8). I was a barren wilderness; nothing grew in me; my soul was empty and void; but now watersprings are bubbling up.' And he began to write his great hymns, the verses and the tunes, and the whole Reformation followed, and all began to sing with him.

It was just through seeing this truth, that salvation desiderates and postulates nothing in us except that we see and recognise and confess our barrenness, our emptiness and our woe. That we cry out to the Lord in our distress, and that we discover that he has done everything that is needed to be done in his only begotten Son in order to deliver us. Full salvation; free salvation; all in Christ.

> *Not the righteous—*
> *Sinners Jesus came to call.*
> Joseph Hart

Do you know that? Had you realised that? Is it not the case that you have not been rejoicing and singing until now because you have never seen that? You have always gone on with that very idea, that as a church member, and as a good person, and as a moral person, and as an imitator of Christ, and an imitator of the saints, you were going to make yourself a Christian. That is the essential and the final fallacy. The answer to it is this: 'He turneth the wilderness into a standing water, and dry ground into watersprings.'

Just turn to him, cry out unto him, and he will answer and reveal to you the full provision even in our Lord and Saviour Jesus Christ. And then you will be ready and glad and eager to receive the invitation of the Psalmist who says, 'Let the redeemed of the LORD say so' (v.2). 'Oh that men would praise the LORD for his goodness, and for his wonderful works to the children of men!' (v.8). Yes, the most wonderful work of all: the work upon the cross.

8
True Christianity

'He turneth the wilderness into a standing water, and dry ground
into watersprings. And there he maketh the hungry to dwell, that
they may prepare a city for habitation; and sow the fields, and
plant vineyards, which may yield fruits of increase. He blesseth
them also, so that they are multiplied greatly; and suffereth not
their cattle to decrease . . . The righteous shall see it, and
rejoice: and all iniquity shall stop her mouth. Whoso is wise,
and will observe these things, even they shall understand
the lovingkindness of the LORD.*'*
(Psalm 107:35-38,42-43)

The Psalmist has given his four pictures, then he has turned to the application, and the final conclusion to which he brings us is in this last verse, verse 43: 'Whoso is wise,' he says, 'and will observe these things, even they shall understand the lovingkindness of the LORD.' In other words, if we have never praised God, if we do not know what it is to have in our hearts a hymn of praise unto God, then there is only one explanation, says this man: it is ignorance. It is a lack of wisdom, which means a lack of knowledge, a lack of understanding, a lack of discrimination and observation.

In other words, the whole attitude of the Bible to any person who is not in the right relationship to God, and who is not worshipping God and praising him, is that such a person is ignorant. The word the Bible actually uses is the word *fool*. 'The fool hath said in his heart, There is no God' (Psalm 14:1). Fool means lacking in knowledge and understanding. Such people do not think;

they do not observe or use their eyes. They do not really make a note of what they see in life and in this world and draw the inevitable deductions and conclusions.

Now that is the whole case of the Bible against such persons, so it comes as a great message to them, asking them to awaken, to begin to look and to see and to observe. But that is the last thing we want to do with regard to these matters, is it not? We all start off with our prejudices and we cling tenaciously to them; or, rather, perhaps I should say that they hold us firmly in their grip in a sort of vice. We cannot escape, and they will not allow us to think; they will not allow us to face the facts. We just go on thoughtlessly.

I think we will all agree with that proposition. We must agree that if all men and women simply sat down and thought first before they acted, life would be very different. I cannot believe that anybody would be deliberately cruel or unkind, or act as a beast, but many are doing so. If many people thought of the suffering they caused, I do not think they would do it. But they do not think, or, at any rate, their thinking is partial and incomplete. They do not observe. They are not wise in this sense and they do not understand. But especially the Psalmist's case is that the only ultimate explanation of why it is that everybody is not worshipping and praising God, is our failure to understand the truth about God.

Now the Bible is a book that seems to be contradicting itself. It tells us on the one hand that all our thinking and all our efforts will never make us Christians and provide salvation for us. But on the other hand, it tells us that if we are lost, it is because we have not thought and because we have not worked and reasoned things out. In other words, it makes the argument that if we really only observed life as it is; if we only worked out the argument, then we would be bound to believe in God.

The Bible tells us that in many ways. Take, for instance, the whole argument from creation. Are you really prepared to believe that flowers, in their variety and in their colour and in their perfection, are but the result of accident and chance? Think of all the constellations and the stars, and all the wonder of the firmament. Think of nature and all its rich variety: the rivers and the mountains, the plains and all the wealth and the variety that you find there. Is all this accidental? The Bible's answer is that God has put his fingerprints in nature, so that as you observe the fingerprints, if you really reason and understand and think, you reason back to the mind that used the fingers (Psalm 8:3).

The apostle Paul says, in the first chapter of the Epistle to the Romans, that we are all without excuse: 'For the invisible things of him from the creation of the world are clearly seen, being understood by the things that are made, even his eternal power and Godhead' (Romans 1:20). Creation is an indication of a creator God who is at the back of it all. But we do not observe; we do not look; we do not think. 'Ah,' we say, 'very nice flowers: they can be bought for such and such a price, or you can pick them in the garden. Marvellous!' And then we stop.

But where do they come from? What is the explanation of it all? That is the kind of argument you find everywhere in the Bible, and it is the argument of the Psalmist at this point. He says, 'If you are not praising God, there is only one reason for it: you are not using your eyes; you do not see what is happening round and about you. Look at life, read the pages of history as well as that of creation, and you will come to certain conclusions.'

Then he gives us, you remember, these astounding results of his own observations. We have already looked at some of them. He says that if we only kept our eyes open and observed, we should very soon be convinced of the greatness and the power of God. Things are not what they seem. You look at life superficially and you think that things go on in their own momentum and that great men determine life. During the Second World War—and before it—we read in the newspapers that the whole of history and the fate of all mankind was in the hands of five men. So it appeared; but that was nonsense. Where are those five men by now? They have gone, they have vanished, they are off the scene. We are almost beginning to forget their very names. Why? Because God has taken them away. He can blow them away with a breath of his mouth. 'He poureth contempt upon princes' (v.40).

We looked at this earlier—the might and the majesty and the greatness of God, God the judge eternal. Those who have read history truly are people who ought to walk softly. O yes, you read history superficially and you talk about Alexander the Great and Julius Caesar and Napoleon and people like that, but their dynasties and their empires have gone crashing to nothingness. Someone once pointed out very rightly that the man whom you and I and the history books call 'Alexander the Great', the book of Daniel calls a 'he goat' (Daniel 8:5), just showing you exactly where such men are and what their true size is.

Use your eyes, says the Psalmist. Can you not see—if you begin to think—that you cannot afford to adopt an independent attitude with God, because your life is in the hands of God? You are here now, but where will you be tomorrow night? You do not know. Our times are in his hands (Psalm 31:15) and 'It is a fearful thing to fall into the hands of the living God' (Hebrews 10:31). 'Reason,' says the Psalmist, 'be wise, observe, see what is happening round and about you. These men who pitted themselves against God, where are they?' But not only that, he tells us that the greatest tragedy of all, in a sense, is that people do not observe God's salvation. Not only are they ignorant of his power and his greatness, they are blind and they are ignorant with respect to what he has done about our deliverance.

Now we have seen already that this salvation of God is altogether different from everything we have ever thought. We saw one other thing: that our salvation does not depend upon us at all, not to the slightest extent. It is entirely the result of what God himself has done in his only begotten Son, our Lord and Saviour Jesus Christ.

Character of salvation

Then the Psalmist tells us that the next thing that we are so blind about by nature, and so fail to observe, is the wonderful nature, the character of this salvation. And he deals with this in these verses 35 to 38 that we are now considering especially. He puts it, of course, in his typical poetic imagery: 'He turneth the wilderness into a standing water, and dry ground into watersprings. And there he maketh the hungry to dwell, that they may prepare a city for habitation; and sow the fields, and plant vineyards, which may yield fruits of increase. He blesseth them also, so that they are multiplied greatly; and suffereth not their cattle to decrease.'

Now the blessings of salvation in the Old Testament are nearly always represented in that material way. There is nothing that so gives us a perfect picture of God's amazing condescension as the way in which he always stoops to the level of the people to whom he is speaking. In the Old Testament he revealed his desire to bless, and his way of doing so was in a material manner, with material prosperity, as depicted here in this picture. But that is only a picture of the same truth, the same message, which we have in a more spiritual form in the New Testament Scriptures. So in this psalm we read, 'He blesseth them also, so that they are multiplied greatly'; while the apostle Paul, in writing to the Ephesians, talks about 'the exceeding riches of his grace' (Ephesians 2:7) or 'the unsearchable riches of Christ' (Ephesians 3:8). It is exactly the same thing, the same God giving a picture in the Old and giving it in its fulness in the New.

So let us now continue with our consideration of the marvellous and the wonderful character of the blessings of this Christian salvation. We have seen that it means forgiveness of sins, but it means much more than that; that is only the beginning.

Work of God

Something amazing follows. What is it? Well, let me try to tell you about it, interpreting this man's pictures. The *first* thing about this great Christian salvation is that it is the work of God in the soul. The Psalmist says, 'He [God] turneth the wilderness into a stand-ing water, and dry ground into watersprings.' This work, therefore, is a miracle. There was this wilderness, and the very last thing you can do with a wilderness is suddenly to make it abound with a great water supply. It was just a barren rocky land where there was no water whatsoever; there was just nothing there at all in any way. But, suddenly, this wilderness becomes standing water, and where there was dry ground which had always presented a problem as far as water was concerned, suddenly you find a mass of watersprings springing up all round. You have done nothing about it yourself, but there it is. It has happened!

This is nothing less than a miracle. A miracle is an action that God alone can perform, a manifestation of his eternal, creative power. It is the God who normally chooses to act through second-ary causes, and by various ways and means, acting directly. It is not that he breaks his laws; he supersedes them for the time being, and, of course, God can always do that. He chooses one way; he can choose another way. He chooses indirect methods; he can choose the direct method. And a miracle is God acting directly, immediately; God producing something out of nothing, as it were; God exerting again his great creative power.

And I am privileged to say to you that when you become a Christian, you are nothing short of a miracle. For anybody to become a Christian is a miracle. That is why it is so difficult for one not to be vehement as one denounces that conception of the Christian as just a good man; a man who is pulling himself up by his own boot strings; a man who is trying to live a good life. If you say that, you are robbing God of his glory, and you do not under-stand the glorious position of the Christian. It is God who has acted upon him or her, and he has acted upon their souls. The Creator has taken hold of them and smashed the old and re-formed the new.

To use the pictures of the Old Testament prophets, it is like a potter taking hold of a lump of clay and forming and fashioning it (Jeremiah 18:2). Yes, to use the further picture, it is of a potter taking hold of a vessel that was a little bit marred, and first of all smashing it, then taking hold of it and moulding it again, and forming it into a new mould after a new pattern. That is what happens when one becomes a Christian. It is a miraculous action; it is the action of the almighty God himself. It is not the man or woman themselves doing it. It is not the preacher persuading them to do something. Indeed, it is not the preacher doing anything. It is God! It is not even the preaching; it is not the philosophy; it is not the theory; it is nothing but the direct action of almighty God himself. A wilderness becoming standing water; dry ground, watersprings.

And, of course, because it is miraculous, it cannot be understood. At least it seems to me that there is something tragically wrong with the mental processes of anyone who tries to understand a miracle. By definition, a miracle cannot be understood. When I postulate that a miracle is the direct action of God, then how can I understand it? How can anybody understand it? It is no use trying to understand the mechanics of how a wilderness becomes standing water. You can try if you like. You can go and consult the geologists, but they will tell you, if they are honest, that they just do not know; that this sort of thing does not happen. I have never seen it before, but I must admit it. I have ocular evidence and demonstration that there is that standing water where I know that formerly there was a wilderness. I just do not know how it happened, and the geologists cannot know because it does not conform to the rules. It is above them. It is supernatural. So is the Christian.

Our blessed Lord himself has given us a perfect exposition of this in the third chapter of John's Gospel. How well we understand Nicodemus! There he is confronted by this man. He has been watching him, he has been listening to him, and, of course, he has been observing, and he has drawn certain conclusions. So he goes to him at night and he says, 'Master, I see and understand clearly that "thou art a teacher come from God: for no man can do these miracles that thou doest, except God be with him"' (John 3:2). Then he was on the point of asking, 'Tell me, how do you do it? What is it you have got? How did you get it? What is this?'

But our Lord interrupts him at once; he is not allowed to put his supplementary questions. 'Verily, verily, I say unto thee, Except a man be born again, he cannot see the kingdom of God' (v.3). 'No, no, I do not understand this,' says Nicodemus. 'It is no use telling me that I, an old man, must be born again. "How can a man . . . when he is old . . . enter the second time into his mother's womb and be born?" It does not sound rational, does it? It does not conform to the usual things that we see in life. It does not conform to the book, as it were. My textbook tells me that this leads to that: cause and effect. But you are talking about being born again, and I am an old man. "How can these things be?"' Poor Nicodemus! Fancy trying to understand a miracle! You cannot do it.

But he goes on, and our Lord at last turns to him and says, 'The wind bloweth where it listeth, and thou hearest the sound thereof, but canst not tell whence it cometh, and whither it goeth' (v.8). Where does it come from? Where is it going? You cannot see it. And everyone who is born of the Spirit is like that. It is beyond our power of analysis. You do not understand it, you simply see its effects and results. You see the clothes on the line waving in the breeze; perhaps when a hurricane comes, a roof is blown off. You still do not understand anything about it. It is a mystery, it is a marvel, it is something beyond us that eludes our grasp. So is everyone who is born of the Spirit.

Is that your conception of being a Christian? Have you realised that that is the very truth about Christian men and women? That there is something about them which is not only incomprehensible

142

to everybody else, but they cannot understand it themselves? They do not know *how* it has happened, but they know that it has. That is all and nothing more. It is like this wind; God's action upon the soul; a miraculous action of the almighty God. When you become a Christian, what will have happened is that God will have taken hold of you and he will have done something within you. That is Christianity. So I do not preach decisions; I preach regeneration; I preach God acting in the souls of men by his Holy Spirit, and nothing else. That is Christianity—the wilderness, standing water; dry ground, watersprings.

Complete change

Then *secondly*—and this follows inevitably from what I have just been saying—the change that God works in the soul is a complete change. You cannot imagine a more complete change than a wilderness and standing water, dry ground and watersprings. It is the complete antithesis. That is what happens to a person when he or she becomes a Christian. It is not just some superficial change; it is not merely something that happens on the surface of life, not a mere superficial improvement, not just an addition to what we already were. Am I making this plain to you? It is an entire change of constitution.

But so many think of Christianity in that superficial way, do they not? They think that when people become Christians, then something happens on the surface. They stop drinking and a few things like that, and there is a superficial change in their conduct and behaviour. They are better men and women. They quit certain things and, perhaps, they add certain things to their lives also. They were good men and women before, but now they become religious people in addition.

But that is not what happens. When God does this work, this miraculous work, he does it in such a way as to change the very constitution. Make your geological analysis of a wilderness. Then make an analysis after it has become standing water, and you will find that it is absolutely different. Go to that dry ground: you have done borings and tests and you see that there is no water there at all. You have called in a water diviner—'Not a trace', he says. There is not a pool, there is nothing anywhere. But go again, and you find that the twig in the hand of the water diviner will not rise up, it is being pulled down. The nature and the constitution of the ground and of the soil is absolutely different. That is becoming a Christian; it is not that people are a little bit better; they have a new nature; it is a complete change.

The apostle Paul tells us that this work of Christ through the Spirit is done 'not in tables of stone, but in fleshy tables of the heart' (2 Corinthians 3:3). When men and women become Christians, it is not the surface of their lives that is changed; it is their hearts. They are given new hearts. They are born again. They become 'a new creature'. They are 'a new man'. Those are the New Testament terms. It is exactly the difference between a wilderness and standing water. Christianity, I repeat, is not mere addition; it is a radical, constitutional change. There was no water there before: it is now full of water. It is as big as that. Something is brought into being in the Christian that was non-existent prior to that. That is Christianity: that the almighty God gives you a gift of life.

When one becomes a Christian, I say, God has almost, as it were, injected this new principle into us so that we really are entirely different people from what we were before. We have a new understanding. Before, we did not understand the Bible at all. We did not understand any of its message. It was a completely boring book. We now begin to understand it. It begins to speak to us. A 'new man' has a new understanding, a new outlook. We have new desires and new tastes. We like the Bible; we like prayer; we like mixing with God's people. Saints used to be utter bores to us: we now prefer their company to anybody in the world, and we would sooner spend the night with the humblest saint in a cottage than dwell in the palaces of kings and queens, if they are not Christians. That is a test of your being a Christian. A new nature demanding new things, having new interests, new hope and new power, in exactly the same way.

Now, let me quote to you something which puts all this much better than I can, and I give you this at random. I could give you thousands of stories to prove the same thing, but I give you this particular one because this book only came into my hand today. This is an account of a man who was a Methodist preacher, who was born at the end of the eighteenth century and who lived into the nineteenth century. Listen to what he says about himself, how he became a Christian.

He says that as the result of what happened to him, 'I could no more doubt of my acceptance with God than of my own existence; and love to God in return for so great and undeserved a benefit sprang up within me.' There was no praise to God before; he was a wilderness. But now, you see, there is praise to God springing up within him. The water has suddenly appeared. 'With a train of spiritual and heavenly affections, mine was a change not only from misery to happiness, from sorrow to joy, but from the love and practice of sin to the love and practice of holiness.'

Then notice: 'The entire bent and habit of my nature was changed.' That is what I am trying to tell you. It is the difference between a wilderness and standing water, between dry ground and watersprings. That is Christianity. When God acts, that is what he does. 'My views and feelings, my apprehensions and inclinations, my desires, hopes and prospects were all new. The experience of nearly 70 years'—he wrote this when he was an old man—'has served only to strengthen my conviction that the change I then underwent was no delusion but a blessed reality, the effect of a divine operation.'

I had prepared my sermon before I read this; but what a perfect statement of it! 'At this moment in 1870, the love of Christ is as sweet as it was on the 16th July 1801, when for the first time, in its richness and power, it was shed abroad in my heart by the Holy Ghost given unto me.' That's it!

Then: 'I returned home from this prayer meeting'—because it happened to him in a prayer meeting—'a distance of about two miles, scarcely knowing whether I was in the body or out of the body; every object in nature above, around, beneath, appeared in an aspect entirely new, and gazing upon the heavens and the earth I felt as I had never felt before the touching sentiment, "My Father made them all."'

Need I say any more? That is what it means to become a Christian. Not your deciding to follow Christ, not your deciding to be better, not your 'going in for Christianity'. No, no! But God putting into you that which so changes you that you really do not know yourself. You are a new person, a new creation. Everything is different. 'Old things are passed away; behold, all things are become new' (2 Corinthians 5:17).

My friend, you must not be satisfied with anything less than this. If you have been satisfied with something less, is it true Christianity, do you think? Are you looking back to your decision, or are you looking back, as Thomas Jackson did, to what God did in his soul and put this new life into him? That is Christianity. And when that happens, it shows itself and you begin to sing and to praise God, and you are lost in a sense of 'wonder, love and praise'. It is a miraculous work. It is a complete work. A complete change.

Satisfying

Then, finally, it is a change that is completely satisfying in its results and effects. Look at the way in which the Psalmist puts it. What is it that one experiences when God does this great work in the soul? Well, the first thing is a sense of rest: 'And there he maketh the hungry to dwell, that they may prepare a city for habitation' (v.36). Before that they had been travelling, they were

146

looking for water and for supplies. They said, 'We would like to settle down somewhere and live a full life, but how can we? We cannot settle down in this wilderness; there is nothing growing here because there isn't any water, so we will die of thirst and of starvation.' But here, everything is changed and they can settle down in 'a city for habitation'. They have found rest for their souls.

There is nothing more blessed about the Christian life than that. It is the end of all the journeyings and the wanderings. Charles Wesley, in the hymn expressing his conversion, asks the question: 'O, when shall all my wanderings cease?' For years you have been looking for something that you cannot find; looking for rest for your soul; looking for peace; looking for happiness. You have read books; you have attended lectures; you have listened to sermons. There is nothing you have not done. There is a longing. You travel backwards and forwards, and you are searching and seeking, but you cannot find. 'O, when shall all my wanderings cease?' And then, suddenly, you find that you have arrived; just when you were most hopeless, you met someone with an eye of pity who said, 'Come unto me, all ye that labour and are heavy laden, and I will give you rest' (Matthew 11:28). And you went to him and you found it.

> *I heard the voice of Jesus say,*
> *Come unto Me and rest;*
> *Lay down, thou weary one, lay down*
> *Thy head upon My breast.*
>
> Horatius Bonar

You heard him, you listened to him, you did it and you found rest for your soul. O, let me utter the great and the memorable phrase of Augustine, the brilliant philosopher. He had been wandering and seeking. At last he heard the voice, he had found it, Christ calling him to rest, and, as it were, he sat down and wrote:

'Thou hast made us for thyself, and our souls are restless until they find their rest in thee.' That city for habitation: the end of the journeyings. You need not prospect for water any longer. It is gushing up before your eyes. Settle down, build your city, find rest for your souls; the end of wandering and striving and vain seeking and searching.

Yes, but not only that, there is satisfaction also. 'He turneth a wilderness into a standing water, and dry ground into watersprings. And there he maketh the hungry to dwell' (vv.35,36). The hunger and thirst of life are satisfied for the first time. You will forgive me, I know, but I find it very difficult to finish with this psalm. I could go on for hours on this: the satisfaction of becoming a Christian.

What am I talking about? Well, I am talking about *intellectual satisfaction.* I assure you that there is no intellectual satisfaction in the whole wide world but this. Here there is complete intellectual rest and satisfaction. I do not speak about myself in this pulpit, but I am a man who by nature is restless, intellectually restless, intellectually inquisitive. I am a born sceptic. I use reason, I believe in reason, and, like Nicodemus, I want to know reasons. I did not find them in the way I expected, but I have found them. They are all here. Intellectual rest. I am interested in the philosophy of history. I am interested in the nature of man, I am interested to know why the world is as it is, and I find no explanation except this. Here I find a complete answer. I know of no problem but that I find the answer here—I am making the statement deliberately—complete intellectual satisfaction.

O yes, but not only intellectual. I find also complete *emotional satisfaction.* I am emotional. I like to be moved. I know of nothing that can move me like this. You know, I find it difficult at times to read certain passages in the Scriptures; they overcome me. There are certain hymns, the words and the tunes: have you not felt them moving you to the very foundations of your being? Oh, not the sentiment of the films, but a strong, healthy emotion that you are never ashamed of afterwards. Something that puts you on your feet, charges you like a battery, makes you feel that you are a superman almost, because of the divine energy! That is what you get when this change takes place: a complete satisfaction intellectually, emotionally, and in every other respect.

But also, you will find that you have *a purpose in life*. The tragedy about men and women who are not Christians is that their lives are purposeless. They do not know where they are going. They do not know what they are doing. The whole of life is uncertain, and that is why they live as they do. They are going round and round in circles and they do not know where it is all going to end. But come to this position and you will see your life in this world as but a journey, but a pilgrimage. The hymn-writer in his hymn could thank God that even the joys of this world are touched with a little pain; that even the most wonderful roses have thorns and pricks upon them. Beauty and pain together. He thanked God for it because all these blessed, happy, joyous things 'may be our guide and not our chain'. They are there, and they are put there by God to remind us that this is not the only life and the only world, but that we are moving on and that we are only pilgrims and strangers and sojourners and travellers.

We are going on to a great and endless eternal life, and there is a purpose in it all: I am here to live to God's glory and to help others, to bring them to the same life in order to safeguard their eternal future. What a wonderful purpose! Life does not become just a riot or a round of pleasure-seeking which ends in pain and remorse and regret. No, no! There is a purpose and an objective. Something leading me ever onwards. That is what happens. And not only that, there is growth and development; sowing the fields and planting vineyards which may yield fruits of increase. 'He blesseth them also, that they are multiplied greatly.'

That is another wonderful thing about this life. It is *a life that grows*. I say this to the glory of God in this pulpit. I know much more about the grace of God today than I did a year ago. There is no end to this. It is like entering into a great sea, and you swim out and you think that you must have reached the greatest depth of all. Not a bit! You are only at the beginning. It is so amazing; it expands the horizon, goes ever further and further away. Or it is like a man climbing a mountain: he thinks he has reached the top, but there is yet another peak before him. The Christian life goes on and the depths are more profound and the heights are greater. My dear friend, you who are not a Christian, do you think this Christian life is boring? No, it is exciting; it is tremendously exciting. I will tell you quite frankly, my greatest problem in this world is to find time. There are so many things I want to read, and so many things I want to do, and I am discovering fresh aspects; its increasing glories come to meet me as I go round fresh corners. It is entering into this eternal scheme and plan of God. 'Grow in grace', says Peter, 'and in the knowledge of our Lord and Saviour Jesus Christ.'

That is Christianity; and nothing less than that. Christians know that, apart from the Lord Jesus Christ and his death for them upon the cross, they are hopeless. They know that they are children of God only in and through Christ. They owe it all to him, so they give him all the praise.

'Let the redeemed of the LORD say so.' Have you said it? Have you praised him? If you have not, and you have now seen the truth about God and his goodness and his wonderful redemption, praise him here and now by yourself. Praise God—and then tell others about him, because if you believe what I am saying you will want everybody to know it. You will see that they are in the same desperate position as you were and that nothing can ever deliver them but this. You will try to bring them also to join with you in this same glorious privilege of being in this choir of the redeemed here upon earth; mingling our voices with the choir of the redeemed above, singing the praises of him who once was slain and has redeemed us to God the Father.

Consider these things as this man in the psalm exhorts you to do, and then begin to give thanks unto the Lord because he is so good, because his mercy endures for ever. It has endured until now. He has kept you alive. He has given you another opportunity. Realise it. Believe it. And begin to give proof of it by praising him with all your soul.